ASTRAL PRO

 a beginner's guide

RICHARD CRAZE

Hodder & Stoughton

A MEMBER OF THE HODDER HEADLINE GROUP

To Mike Jay
without whose help, research and advice
this book would never have happened.
Thank you, Mike.

Order queries: please contact Bookpoint Ltd, 39 Milton Park, Abingdon, Oxon
OX14 4TD. Telephone: (44) 01235 400414, Fax: (44) 01235 400454. Lines are open
from 9.00–6.00, Monday to Saturday, with a 24-hour message answering service.
Email address: orders@bookpoint.co.uk

British Library Cataloguing in Publication Data
A catalogue record for this title is available from The British Library

ISBN 0 340 73755 7

First published 1996
This edition published 1999
Impression number 10 9 8 7 6 5 4 3 2 1
Year   2004 2003 2002 2001 2000 1999

Typeset by Transet Limited, Coventry, England.
Printed in Great Britain for Hodder & Stoughton Educational, a division of Hodder
Headline plc, 338 Euston Road, London NW1 3BH by Cox and Wyman Limited,
Reading, Berks.

CONTENTS

Chapter 4   Practical techniques of astral projection   59

Useful information   89

INTRODUCTION

When I first started to collect the research necessary to write this book a lot of the people along the way seemed to have very definite views about what astral projection is – or rather isn't. Roughly they could be divided into three groups:

- Those who thought astral projection was something esoteric and probably to do with magic or ritual;
- Those who thought it was an old expression that had been replaced by the more current 'Near Death Experience' (NDE) or 'Out of the Body Experience' (OOBE);
- Those who said that it was something dangerous and that a friend of a friend (never someone that they actually knew themselves, of course) had suffered some trauma or spirit experience where he or she had been attacked by entities of some sort.

Dispelling myths

What I have tried to do in this book is to dispel all the myths surrounding astral projection.

- Astral projection has nothing whatever to do with magic or religion or any belief system. It involves no rituals or paraphernalia. It is an investigation into a subject that has intrigued and fascinated people for thousands of years. I will offer no conclusions as to whether it's a viable proposition, and no guarantees that you will achieve anything. What I will do is present the evidence for astral projection along with the techniques that have been recommended over a very long period

1

of time as being those which are the most likely to achieve some measure of success.

- Astral projection is a conscious effort or attempt to produce an Out of the Body Experience – a controlled experiment, if you like. OOBEs tend to happen relatively spontaneously without any will or control exercised by the person to whom the experience happens. NDEs happen when someone is on the point of dying and is resuscitated.
- I have never encountered evidence to suggest that astral projection is in any way dangerous or even mildly risky. There is simply no evidence to suggest that anyone has ever suffered adverse or ill effects from trying to produce an astral projection under natural conditions. Anyone foolish or dangerous enough to attempt similar effects using hallucinogenic drugs, and who has suffered any harm, should blame the drugs not the experience.

So what is astral projection?

Well, we will go into more detail in subsequent chapters but, put simply, it is an attempt to have an experience of being outside the human body while conscious and alive and, preferably, awake. There are certain related experiences which can happen while a person is conscious but asleep – these occur during lucid dreams, which we will cover later.

How is it done?

Again, we will go into more detail later, but suffice to say that there seems to be a part of the human being which is capable of existing – albeit for short periods of time – outside the body. The problem then arises as to what to call this part – soul, spirit, astral body, spirit form, shadow matter. You can see the problem: each of these has a whole mountain of connotations around it. However, hopefully, we can overcome the prejudices later on. This life force can be encouraged to leave the body under certain conditions (sometimes it

can even be tricked). Some techniques work for some people and others for other people. I have collected and presented as many as possible so that you can try any you consider suitable for you. I have tried to avoid any of the more bizarre or complex and stuck to the simple, safe and practical techniques.

Why would anyone want to have an astral projection?

- Some people find it immensely reassuring – if their life force can exist outside the body during life it seems, to them, to be self-evident that life after death is not just a possibility but a demonstrable fact.
- Others use the techniques to promote or deepen their own experience of spirituality – a sort of religious experience where they find a harmony and understanding of the universe and their own part within it.
- For others it's a sort of attempt to prove that astral projection isn't possible – a cynical denial of any form of continuation of life after the death of the human body; sometimes these people succeed by not succeeding – they don't achieve an experience of astral projection despite trying, which reinforces their own belief in their lack of belief.
- Others attempt to learn all about astral projection to use it as a tool for clairvoyance, increasing extrasensory perception (ESP), or even some form of sophisticated spying (there is information in Chapter 2 about the CIA experiments into astral projection).
- Some people are just natural-born finders-out – suggest something and they'll have to try it just to see if it's possible.

Which category are you? There are no wrong or right answers. The techniques are easily available to anyone, and whatever your reasons for reading this book and attempting astral projection, the experience may well change your initial reasons. I started out as a finder-out and have ended up as a committed believer in life after death because of my experiences.

Scientific research

I have also included as much relevant scientific research as possible to begin to explore the idea that science and spirit are increasingly working in harmony – no bad thing – and also to indicate that some of these experiences are clinically proven; they can be measured, weighed and observed.

The evidence for astral projection

This book explores the evidence for astral projection, both historically and practically, defines and examines OOBEs and NDEs; and includes some case histories to give you an idea of what other people have experienced. There is no guarantee that your experience will be anything like theirs.

Whether or not you are successful in your attempts at astral projection remains to be seen, but perhaps if we lose sight of the goal, we may enjoy the journey more. Our success may not be measured in our achievement but in the insights gained along the way. One thing you will find about astral projection and all that surrounds it is that you will end up knowing yourself a whole lot better mentally, emotionally and spiritually.

And please work your way through this book properly – no cheating and turning straight to the chapter on techniques. You'll need a thorough grounding in the background before you're ready for that.

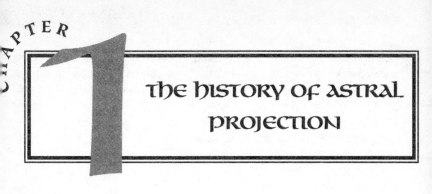

The bistory of astral projection

The ancient Egyptians were probably the first culture to record and write down their beliefs about the soul. They recorded in hieroglyphics inscribed in tombs hundreds of prayers to be read aloud over the recently deceased to guide the soul or spirit on its journey to the next life. These prayers have been collected and form the Egyptian Books of the Dead. *From these prayers we find that the ancient Egyptians divided the universe into three – Heaven, Earth and the Duat, the next-world. The Duat, sometimes known as Amenti, was where the sun god, Ra, went each evening when he departed from the sky.*

Ancient beliefs

The cult of Osiris

The cult of Osiris flourished in the Nile valley, and followers of Osiris believed that when they died they had to stand before him and have their heart weighed on the Scales of Judgement against the Feather of Truth. The jackal-headed god, Anubis, did the weighing and Thoth, the baboon-headed god, recorded the result. If they failed the weighing, which they would do if they had failed to follow the forty-two commandments of Ra, they were thrown to Am-mut – the Eater of the Dead – part lion, part crocodile and part hippo. If they passed they stayed in paradise with Osiris for ever in the Fields of Peace and were known as *maa-kheru* – the victorious (The Greeks later took this theme further with their Elysian Fields.)

The Egyptians believed that the soul, the *ba*, was housed in a spirit body, the *Ka*. This was usually represented as a human with a bird's head (often a hawk). The ba was known as the heart-soul and was deemed to be everlasting and incorruptible. The Ka, however, was a spirit body which exactly duplicated the living body and, on death, gave way to the *sahu*, the true spirit body which would house the ba for ever. During life the Ka and the sahu were one and the same thing and only after death did the Ka slowly diminish until only the sahu remained with its soul.

The Egyptians believed that during life the Ka was capable of leaving the body. They often drew pictures of this as a human body asleep with the Ka floating above it in a way reminiscent of modern descriptions of NDEs.

ANCIENT GREEK BELIEFS

The Greeks had a concept of a 'double body' which housed the soul. Plato believed that the spirit could leave the body during life and that the physical world would then be seen only dimly, as if through mist. He thought that the soul was imprisoned in its human form and would become free upon death. Both Aristotle and Plotinus taught that the spirit could leave the body and were capable of being separated during life from their physical body.

Homer believed that we are made up of three parts: the physical body, the *soma*; the astral body, the *psyche*; the spirit itself, the *thumos*. He said that the psyche was not an astral body as we think of it but rather a life principle which had an exact double, the *eidolon*, which manifested during dreams.

The cult of Dionysus practised a particularly horrid ritual where they tore a live bull to pieces with their teeth, and ran through the woods naked and shouting and working themselves into a state of hysteria. This all took place at night along with the noise of drums and cymbals and extremely agitated dancing. This induced state of mania they called *ekstasis* which means 'outside of the body'. They believed that by following this 'ecstasy' they could achieve *enthousiasmos*, union with god.

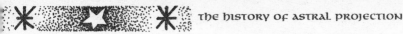

TIBETAN BELIEFS

The Tibetans have taken knowledge of the astral body to an extraordinary degree. They believe that on death the soul is housed in the *bardo* body and they read prayers over the recently dead for forty-nine days as the bardo body makes its journey to the next incarnation. These prayers were all collected and written down in the eighth century AD in the *Tibetan Book of the Dead* which closely parallels the Egyptian equivalent. The bardo body is capable of leaving the human form during life and it is also capable of passing through physical matter as it is composed of psychic material only. The Tibetans claim that the bardo body is capable of being transported instantly to wherever the human host wills it.

CROSS-CULTURAL BELIEFS

Cultures which have no contact with each other and are separated by both distance and time have come up with almost identical ideas about the spirit leaving the body. For example, the Yanomamo Indians of South America, who have been known to the Western world for only the past few decades, have evolved beliefs that their *shamans* (wise men or priests) can leave the body during trance and travel to the astral world, the *hedu*. The soul or spirit is housed in an astral body called *No Borebo* which disintegrates on cremation of the body allowing the spirit to become free, and it then becomes *No Uhudi*, an innocent one and is free to wander through the forest for ever in perfect peace.

Dean Sheils, in research published in the *Journal of the Society for Psychical Research* in 1978 as 'A Cross-cultural Study of Beliefs in Out-of-the-Body Experiences', compared the belief systems of over sixty different cultures and found that fifty-four of them had some concept of astral projection or astral travel and that half of them also believed that it is possible for this to happen consciously and while alive. Almost half claimed that there were certain members of their cultures who could do this at will. Only three cultures seemed to have no concepts or beliefs about this subject. Those that did

believe, on the whole seemed to accept it as a normal and natural part of human existence.

Theosophy

It would seem that the subject of astral projection has been reported by other cultures in very similar ways over the last few thousand years, but the person who is probably most responsible for both the popularity and current terminology of astral projection is Madame Blavatsky. She was Russian and founded the Theosophical Society in New York in 1875 as a vehicle to put forward her own, somewhat unconventional, ideas which she called *theosophy*. This simply was a collection of ideas she had gathered from travels in India, Tibet, and Egypt which she combined with various other spiritual texts. She propounded her philosophy which is that humans are composed of seven bodies all occupying the same space and each getting 'finer' as you get closer to the centre. Her analogy is that these bodies are like outer clothes which can be shed to reveal the true person within.

We will deal with only two of her bodies here: the physical body composed of flesh and blood, and its neighbouring body, which Madame Blavatsky called the *etheric double*. We'll call it the astral body.

Madame Blavatsky thought of the astral body as being composed of energy – or physical vitality – which was not immortal but was constantly reabsorbed into each successive body as the soul was reincarnated. As the astral body was reabsorbed it was regenerated in some way. The astral body was needed both to house the soul and to be a vehicle in which the 'astral world' could be visited. Apparently, according to Madame Blavatsky, we need the 'etheric eyes' that this body has in order to see.

Madame Blavatsky's ideas have formed the fundamental Western concepts about astral projection for the last hundred years. They do, however, contain many aspects which are both ridiculous and contradictory. It may be useful to cover them just so we can gain an

historical viewpoint. Traditionally the human body has been known as the 'gross body' and the 'astral body' is considered as an exact double or replica of the physical body. The astral body is supposed to be composed of etheric matter or material which is vibrating at a higher rate than physical matter.

The astral body, while contained in the physical body, still 'leaks' out slightly and this, when seen by those who claim to be able to do so, is known as the aura. The aura, depending on its colour, appearance and extension, can be used to glean certain information about individuals such as their health, emotional state and spiritual advancement. The aura can be seen all around the physical body extending from a few centimetres up to several metres depending on various factors.

The astral body is supposed to be able to separate from the physical body under certain conditions and enter the 'astral world' which is supposed to be an exact replica of the world of physical matter. The astral world is supposed to contain various 'entities' that can be summoned and used by those who are either trained or in some way qualified to do so. These entities can then be put to use. The astral world is also supposed to contain the *akashic* records which are kept for each human individual and are supposed to be a record of all their activities while alive – a sort of karmic stocktaking of deeds. There are some people who claim to be able to travel in the astral world and access anyone's akashic record.

Traditionally it has been believed that every person, every night, astrally travels. Their astral body is supposed to leave the physical body during sleep. In most cases the astral body does little except rise above the sleeping form and hover there during the night. This process is supposed to be a sort of 'recharging' and is necessary for maintaining health and mental stability. Anyone deprived of sleep for long periods will quickly suffer – not from the lack of sleep but from a form of astral psychosis, because the astral body has been unable to recharge. This astral travel undertaken while asleep is rarely, if ever, remembered because it is done unconsciously by the individual. We do, however, retain some memory of the astral rejoining the physical, and traditionally this is the explanation given

for falling or flying dreams which we have probably all had at some time or another.

According to the theosophists the astral body is made up of ectoplasm which is a form of material drawn from the spirit world. Ectoplasm can also be used by entities to create bodies for themselves. You need to have etheric sight to be able to see ectoplasm which is why most people can't see the astral body hovering above the physical body of someone asleep.

Anyone who bothers to learn to astrally project consciously can, according to tradition, then travel through the astral world while leaving the physical body behind. Theosophists believe that a tenuous link between these two bodies exists – a thin silver cord, infinitely stretchable and infinitely strong – which keeps the physical body alive while the astral body is off on its travels. The breaking of this silver cord is supposed to result in the death of the individual. It seems likely that this silver cord may well have been a bit of invention by the theosophists as it rarely appears in accounts of astral travel from other cultures.

However, most people report little in the way of an astral body and even fewer have reported a cord – silver or any other etheric colour. It seems likely that Blavatsky mixed up a whole lot of ideas and produced a sort of catch-all philosophy that bore little relationship to reality. The trouble with most of the theosophists' ideas about astral travel is that they simply don't fit in with people's experience nor do they make much sense. The whole notion of a silver cord that can stretch indefinitely simply doesn't seem possible, nor do the ideas about ectoplasm or entities. Most of the ideas now seem to belong to an earlier age of Victorian table rapping and spirit manifestations. What may well be needed is a more pragmatic approach based on sound common sense and personal experience.

The best approach to any form of astral projection is to keep an open mind and not be swayed by other people's ideas. What *you* see and experience is a million times more valid than anything you can read about from someone else. Theosophists also believed that if your experience didn't fit in with their theories then it was always you who was wrong – the theory was inviolate. If you failed to see

or experience things in their way, it must be you who was somehow unfit or not spiritually advanced enough to appreciate the subtleties of their order of things. In fact, the last two of the seven bodies that they described were of such a high spiritual value that they were beyond the understanding of us poor mortals and could be known about only by the upper echelons of the theosophist hierarchy.

Animism

The other traditional point of view about astral projection is taken by the school of thought known as the animistic. They go to the other end of the spectrum from the theosophists and believe that the astral body is composed of nothing at all but is, in fact, the spirit of the human individual. The spirit is capable of leaving the body during life and leaves it permanently at death. According to them it's all quite natural and universal and there is nothing spiritual or wondrous about any of it – it's just a simple but little-known part of life. Animists don't really subscribe to the view that the spirit can be consciously projected from the physical body – indeed they seem to profess no desire to know if it's possible, nor any need to try it. Unfortunately, under their rather strict concepts they can lump together a whole range of other phenomena, such as ghosts, and explain them as being a part of natural life – there's nothing to know or explain.

Other Theories

Another theory about astral projection is that it is some sort of mental aberration brought on by external factors such as tiredness, stress, drugs, trauma or shock. This theory is fine until someone else reports seeing a projection of someone at a time or in a place in which he or she could not be physically present. We will look at these cases in more depth in later chapters. The other problem with explaining OOBEs as a mental state is that sometimes people,

especially under scientifically controlled conditions, can see and report information that they would be physically incapable of accessing in their physical bodies. Too many people have had experiences that simply cannot be explained by the 'mental state' theory.

For the last forty-five years there has been a new and more scientific approach to the whole area of astral projection, OOBEs and NDEs. The first major work was done in 1951 by Muldoon and Carrington, who collected and collated over 100 cases of OOBEs. This followed on from their own work on astral projection which they had published in 1929 (see 'Further reading'). They found that their research did indicate that there was a 'double' and that it was capable of existence outside of the human body consciously and that it did somehow survive the death of the individual.

Robert Crookall has written many books on astral projection and covered an amazing amount of research. His research on OOBEs studying a considerable number of people drawn from a wide variety of classes and ethnic origins indicates various recurring themes including:

- some form of double
- a white light or illumination
- the ability to travel at will
- the inability to move or use material objects
- feelings of tranquillity and detachment
- a 'clear' consciousness of what is happening
- a sense of 'realness'.

He also found that these recurring similarities happened no matter what type of OOBE was being experienced or how it was brought about – and he found that there were five basic situations likely to bring about such an effect. They are:

1 an OOBE brought about by a NDE due to illness or exhaustion;
2 an OOBE brought about by a NDE due to accident;
3 an OOBE brought about deliberately by techniques such as are described in later chapters;
4 an OOBE brought about by the application of drugs such as anaesthetics;

5 an OOBE brought about by a trauma or shock.

He also found that there were two distinct types of OOBEs:

1 the enforced kind where the individual would be aware and even see clearly his or her physical body;
2 the deliberate kind where the individual would not be aware or able to see clearly, if at all, his or her physical body.

Crookall thought this to be evidence of life after death, and that at the point of death an individual would have a 'natural' OOBE and thus really have to see clearly his or her physical form to be made aware that they were 'dead' and could then 'move on' in peace. However, the 'unnatural' OOBE was somehow forced and thus the individual would have a cloudy vision of his or her physical form because he or she was not meant to see it – the individual was not yet properly dead.

Before we conclude this chapter on the historical aspects of astral projection it is worth noting that some cultures interpret dreams as evidence of astral travel and others accept or report that shamans can usually undertake astral travel at will, either by taking hallucinogenic drugs or entering trance states. Some cultures believe that the soul or spirit travels through the physical world, and others that astral travel takes place only through the astral world, which is not normally accessible by humans in their physical form. Some cultures accept a belief in both systems.

There are also beliefs about 'travelling clairvoyance' which is where the individual can visit a distant place and observe events there without actually leaving his or her body – what goes out to observe and returns is never satisfactorily explained. This is sometimes known as ESP projection. Both these terms have now been replaced with 'remote viewing' by modern psychics, but no further explanations of the mechanics of such an experience have been provided.

Some cultures report OOBEs as religious experiences and believe them to happen spontaneously and only when the individual is in a 'state of grace'.

Modern physiologists mostly believe that astral projection or anything

like it is purely a mental state which can be explained by complex chemical reactions that are taking place in the brain of the person who thinks he or she is having an OOBE. They have even coined a name for the astral double – they call it an 'autoscopic hallucination' and classify it as a form of mild schizophrenia. However, clever scientific explanations still don't answer the many cases where the projector has either gathered information physically unobtainable or been seen by a third party.

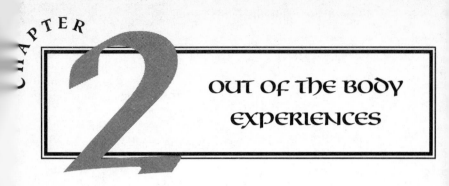

OUT OF THE BODY EXPERIENCES

*A*n OOBE is a modern way of saying astral projection, although it *implies a degree of randomness about the experience. True astral projection is a conscious and controlled attempt to have an experience of the spirit or life force outside of the human body while awake and aware.*

An OOBE is something many people have experienced – often without any warning or previous knowledge that such things could happen.

What is an OOBE?

An OOBE is usually a brief and strange experience that an individual has where the consciousness seems, for sometimes merely a moment or two, to be outside of the body. The individual may or may not be aware of the physical body and often has no experience of the separation of the two – the physical and the conscious. His or her perception of the world is definitely from a viewpoint other than his or her own physical body. The individual may experience something – a conversation overheard or seeing something – that reinforces understanding of the experience. Later he or she remains convinced that what was experienced really was an OOBE. Personal religious or spiritual or psychological beliefs or opinions may well not fit in with the experience. Nevertheless, the strength of the experience and its obvious 'realness' may be stronger than any previously held ideas.

What happens afterwards?

The aftermath of an OOBE is often a sense of newly awakened consciousness – everything has to be questioned and a new world-view has to be formed in the light of the new information acquired. It can be an unsettling experience if you are not expecting it to happen, or have a profound belief that it can't, shouldn't or won't happen. The experience can be so 'real' that the person who has experienced it cannot believe that it isn't more widely known about or even discussed. It is sometimes the case that the person will soon learn to keep quiet about it because of the likely reaction from friends or family who have not experienced such a thing.

How common are OOBEs?

They happen more frequently and to more people than you may think. Sufficient research has now been done, and enough surveys compiled to begin to gauge just how common they are. It would seem from the work so far done that between 5 and 10 per cent of people have had an OOBE. That could be as many as nearly six million people in the United Kingdom and nearly thirty million people in the United States!

Further statistics indicate that around 85 per cent of people who have reported an OOBE say that it occurred while they were resting or trying to sleep. Quite a large proportion had experienced such an event while they were in bed, and a considerable number reported just such an experience while they were either ill or recovering from illness. A small but significant number reported that their experience had occurred while under medication of some sort.

Pilots and bikers

There are a few cases when an OOBE has occurred due to some experience of high-speed travelling. Motor cyclists have reported

this, as have aircraft pilots. For some reason the effect of speed and a floating or flying sensation can seem to trigger an OOBE. It may well be that the curious effect of the sensory stimulation caused by such technology may activate the experience. Some pilots have even reported finding themselves somehow outside of their aeroplane and trying to get back in while being aware that they were still flying the plane. None of the research has indicated any accidents due to this effect. Nor have any surveys reported any feelings of panic or fear at such events – it seems, at the time, quite natural, and only later, upon reflection, is the strangeness or unnaturalness of the experience realised.

Being out and being seen

The surveys conducted have also reported a number of cases where people have had an OOBE in which they have travelled to another place and have been seen there by somebody else. Later the other person has confirmed that he or she saw the person who appeared to them to be physically normal in all respects, and at no time did the observer ever suspect that what he or she was seeing was a form of 'apparition' or astral double. There have even been cases where the observer had a conversation with the out of the body person, which they have both been able to confirm later as being identical.

Natural and voluntary OOBEs

Surveys and reports do seem to indicate a considerable difference between spontaneous OOBEs and deliberate attempts to achieve such an effect (called voluntary OOBEs). The main differences are:

- spontaneous OOBEs may report a bodily shape of some sort, usually an exact double of their physical body;

- most voluntary OOBEs report having a bodily shape which had the attributes of being able to be altered – shape, size, texture and spatial position – at will;
- a considerable number of voluntary OOBEs report some type of joining to their physical body such as the typical 'silver cord'.

Explaining the differences

These differences cannot be satisfactorily explained except by reasoning that the spontaneous 'natural' OOBEs usually occur to people who have little experience of such phenomena – they have no preconceived notions of what to expect, and thus what happens is entirely within the bounds of their knowledge. Voluntary or controlled OOBEs are usually undertaken by people experimenting with the subject. It is likely that they will have read a lot about astral projection and have some expectations based on other people's accounts.

The similarities

There are, however, also considerable similarities between the two types of experience. They are:

- a heightened sense of hearing and sight – colours and lights are brighter and sound is clearer
- strange sounds that couldn't be explained – often loud bangs
- an increased sense of energy and vitality
- a sense of extreme 'realness' to the experience
- an altered sense of 'vibration' of the consciousness
- a subsequent change in their opinions or beliefs about such events and a far greater tendency to accept such an experience as both possible and valid.

After the experience – either voluntary or spontaneous – it seems that the person who has had the experience is much more likely to believe in a life after death. The experience is usually so strong, so realistic, that he or she is utterly convinced that it has happened.

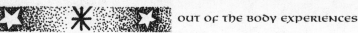

People who have had such an experience are unable to accept that it might be a hallucination, dream, altered mental state or any other explanation. It has happened and it was real – to them. When people relate such an experience it has been found that it is better to accept their understanding of its reality than to try to convince them that they suffered some form of delusion. One of the strongest and most lasting effects is that the experience retains its sense of 'realness' indefinitely. Even after many years have passed the person who had the experience will not question its validity – it happened, it was real, to them, and that conviction does not get shaken by the passing of time.

No matter how hard we try to convince the person who has had an OOBE that what he or she has actually had is some experience of psychic phenomena, we will fail. Commonly, any definition of an OOBE will take this into account. The experience may take many forms – with a body shape or without, for example – but the sense of 'realness' is one of the most enduring qualities. We may not yet be able to prove scientifically or measure such events, but to the person who has experienced an occurrence no proof is needed – he or she *knows* what was experienced.

A typical OOBE

If we try to define what an OOBE is, we need to identify what constitutes such an event. In the majority of cases the similarities reported are sufficient to be able to describe what might be called a 'typical' or 'average' OOBE:

- It usually happens only once in a lifetime. This is true for most spontaneous or 'natural' out of the body experiences. Obviously, people trying to generate the event deliberately are much more likely to have repeat occurrences.
- It is most likely to happen while lying down, either resting or just before or just after sleeping. There have been many cases, however, of OOBEs occurring while carrying out an activity of some kind.
- A floating, flying or soaring feeling usually accompanies the

experience with a certain directional attitude of 'going upwards'.

- Being close to and seeing (or at least being aware of) the physical body – often from above.
- Most cases happen during adult life and most often to women. If an OOBE has occurred during childhood the person is much more likely in later life to attempt deliberate projections.
- Usually there is no sensation of 'leaving' the body. The person just 'finds themselves out'. Return to the physical body is similar, with little sensation or knowledge of 'going back'. Those who attempt deliberate projections are much more likely to report sensations of leaving or returning, but that may well be in the nature of some of the techniques themselves (see Chapter 4).
- A 'usual' case includes no connection physically with the physical body.
- A sense of 'realness' and viewing the 'normal' world – there are few cases reported of leaving the room or area around the physical body.
- The senses of sight and hearing seem to work quite normally, but few cases are reported of experiencing taste, smell or touch. The sight and hearing may well be enhanced or exaggerated, and many cases have reported objects 'glowing' or radiating increased light in some way.
- An initial OOBE is usually accompanied by feelings of detachment, calm and feeling 'OK' – often quite pleasant. Later deliberate projections may be more likely to be subject to fear, apprehension or excitement.
- The person usually feels that the experience is real and at no time does he or she question what is being experienced. There is often a feeling of being able to 'go anywhere' and 'do anything', but the need to do so is rarely felt.
- An inability to affect, move or influence any physical objects in the vicinity of the physical body – and no desire to do so.

Who has OOBEs?

Different research has thrown up different results – any number from 5 per cent to 10 per cent of people claim to have experienced

an OOBE (although some surveys put the figure as high as 14 per cent). However, one interesting result thrown up is that if you are a student you are much more likely than any other section of the population to have had an OOBE. Why this should be no-one can really explain. There also seems to be a connection between 'soft' drug use and OOBEs, but that may be because the hallucinogenic properties of some drugs such as marijuana have a tendency to 'loosen' the consciousness and increase the likelihood of an OOBE occurring. The increased occurrence of OOBEs amongst students may well be related to lifestyle and interests – students are, by their very nature, inquisitive and keen to explore. They are more likely to have heard or read about OOBEs and are more adventurous or interested to experiment and attempt the experience than older people who may be more set in their ways and beliefs. Deliberate or voluntary cases are much more often reported amongst the young than spontaneous cases.

It has also been found that one's religious beliefs have absolutely no bearing on the results – OOBEs affect all races, belief systems and cultures, all age groups, sexes and social backgrounds.

Repeating the experience

Anyone who has had an OOBE is much more likely to want to repeat the experience, but not many actually do so, despite quite rigorous attempts. However, anyone who has had a spontaneous OOBE and then attempted a voluntary OOBE with any degree of success, is likely to be able to repeat the experience. There is a certain 'mind-set' necessary for success – once that approach has been learnt or discovered it's much more likely to produce positive results in subsequent attempts. The experience of having had a spontaneous, unplanned OOBE does not give the recipient any particular knowledge that can subsequently be used – the whole process has to be learnt from scratch, but there is definitely an incentive to want to produce subsequent projections consciously.

Whatever one's beliefs before a spontaneous or voluntary OOBE,

there seems to be a radical and permanent change in one's attitude to the soul, death, and life after death. The fear of death seems to reduce markedly and 95 per cent of those who have had one OOBE said that they wanted another. This seems to indicate that it is both pleasurable and rewarding.

Is it all a dream?

The answer would seem to be most definitely not. The common characteristics of dreams is that they are unlike 'real' life, they are often difficult to remember, recall of them fades quickly, one's consciousness is vague and uncontrolled, and they happen when we are asleep. OOBEs on the other hand are characterised by their 'realness', the ease with which they are remembered – often more vividly than any other single event in a person's life – recall of them doesn't fade in any way with time, the individual's consciousness is total and often heightened and enhanced, and OOBEs most often happen while the person is awake – albeit sleepy, relaxed or medicated.

What's the scientific evidence?

Volunteers who have claimed to be able to generate OOBEs at will have been clinically tested, and various interesting results have been found. During a reported OOBE the equipment that the volunteer has been 'wired-up' to – an electroencephalograph (EEG) machine – has shown that their alpha waves decrease in activity while their beta waves increase. These changes in brain-wave activity are important. There are sixteen principal brain waves, of which we are interested only in the first four:

- Delta waves (1–4 hertz) produced during deep sleep;
- Theta waves (5–7 hertz) produced on the point of sleep and in certain hypnogogic states;
- Alpha waves (8–12 hertz) produced when someone is resting quietly, but disappearing when the eyes are opened or when

 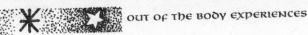

precise mental activity, such as mental arithmetic, is taking place;

- Beta waves (13–30 hertz) produced during normal activity while awake. Obviously waves at the lower end of the range (13) are produced by calmer moods than those at the upper end (30) produced in states of extreme agitation.

The EEG instruments are monitored by electrodes placed on the volunteer's scalp, and these electrodes record the electrical potential of the cerebral cortex.

Sleep and dreams

When we sleep – in delta or theta – we have two types of sleep: paradoxical sleep, where we produce Rapid Eye Movements (REM) and where we do most of our dreaming; and orthodox sleep (NREM), where we barely dream. Orthodox sleep occupies about 80 per cent of our sleep and occurs in periods of about 100 minutes. Then we have a brief period – 10 to 20 minutes on average – of paradoxical sleep (about 20 per cent of total sleep) and then back to orthodox sleep for another 100 minutes. This process goes on all night. If you wake someone in or immediately after paradoxical sleep, they will usually have good memory recall of their dreams. If as little as five minutes has elapsed before they are woken they will have little or no memory of their dreams. Paradoxical sleep is around 1 hertz and orthodox sleep 2 to 4 hertz, although these are both classified as delta waves.

The other monitored body activities are heart rate, respiration rate, REMs and the skin electrical resistance potential (SERPs) of electrodermal activity.

Monitored results

From monitored volunteers who claim to be able to project at will, the following results have been observed (these are average interpretations):

- Alpha waves decrease, indicating a relaxed and calm state;
- Beta waves increase, indicating the volunteer is 'awake';
- Electrodermal activity falls, indicating increased relaxation;
- Heart rate increases, indicating the presence of some activity or stimulus;
- Respiration rate increases, indicating some activity or stimulus;
- REM is absent, although there are more eye movements than in orthodox sleep – there are no theta or delta waves, indicating the volunteer is not asleep or dreaming.

Interpreting the findings

The findings seem to indicate a volunteer in a relaxed state, but with a considerable degree of alertness. They are not asleep. There is no abrupt change in brain waves such as one would expect with the onset of sleep; changes occur gradually.

What do the tests prove?

They indicate that something is going on – some physical changes can be recorded and studied, but obviously more evidence is needed. Instead of just monitoring the volunteers' physical changes, tests have been set up whereby the only way they could acquire certain information is by actually projecting. In one series of tests a male volunteer was cued by the sound of a bell to tell him when to start projecting. A seven-figure number was displayed in the next room only after the bell was rung. After a suitable interval the number was hidden again and the bell sounded to tell the volunteer to 'return' to his physical body. The results were, not surprisingly, unpredictable. In most cases, the attempts proved futile. However, on one occasion the volunteer managed to get the first six digits of the number completely correct – both the numbers and their order.

In another series of tests, a female volunteer was given a complicated picture to try to 'see'. The picture was arranged so that she couldn't see it from where she was lying, and it was also

'fragmented' so that her viewpoint had to change several times to be able to see the entire picture. Again the results were varied and, in most attempts, disappointing. On two separate occasions, however, the volunteer was able not only to 'see' the entire picture but she reported conversations taking place in the next room about the tests which she would have been unable to overhear from her position during the tests.

Another volunteer, while 'projecting', saw and later described a visitor who had arrived after the volunteer was wired up to the EEG. The visitor remained out of sight of the volunteer and left before the test was completed. The description fitted the partner of one of the technicians, who had indeed arrived and departed while the volunteer was being tested. The volunteer had never met or seen the person and had no prior knowledge about the visit.

In one series of tests some forty volunteers had half ping-pong balls placed over their eyes. This, in effect, gave them what is known as a visual ganzfield – they could keep their eyes open and be aware of light but 'see' absolutely nothing. Half the volunteers were asked to attempt to leave their bodies and project to the next room to see a target object. The other half were asked to do nothing except relax and imagine they were projecting. The results were quite interesting, if a little disappointing. Over half of the projecting group reported a feeling of being out of their bodies compared with only four of those who were asked not to. Those who felt that they had projected were quite definite about the target object, while those staying behind were vague and unsure – they admitted they were guessing. However, both groups 'scored' the same – exactly what one would expect for chance or random guesses.

Further testing using other methods such as getting the volunteers to close their eyes, providing mechanical apparatus that simulated floating, and getting volunteers to listen to taped instructions, have all produced results the same as those produced by chance. Volunteers have reported the sensations of projecting and their EEGs have indicated something going on, but they have been unable to back up their claims with demonstrable proof of retrieved information. Perhaps more research is needed in this field.

Lucid dreams

There is a certain type of dream – known as lucid dreams – where the experience seems very real and one is aware of one's consciousness, and often the fact that one is dreaming. There is a considerable body of opinion that says that lucid dreaming is an attempt by the dreamer to interpret an astral projection in a way that makes sense. There is also another school of thought that dismisses the whole notion of astral projection as being nothing more than lucid dreaming. However, the evidence, fragmentary as it is, from EEG readings seems to indicate that the two experiences are different. Lucid dreaming is usually accompanied by REM, delta waves and slowed heart and respiratory rates identical with normal paradoxical sleep. OOBEs are usually accompanied by NREM, an absence of delta waves indicating that the subject is not asleep, an increase in beta waves indicating that the subject is awake, increased pulse and respiratory rates indicating arousal of some sort, and bodily activity. Physiologically the two effects are quite different.

Is it a hallucination?

The mental state necessary for a hallucination is similar to that required for an OOBE. Physiologically, the two effects are difficult to tell apart: both have a sense of realness; both have heightened sense of vision and hearing; both can be accompanied by visual effects that go beyond the 'normal'; both are little understood and regarded as somehow 'abnormal'; both can be brought on by drugs or medication. However, there does seem to be one real difference – the perception of the person experiencing the effect. Someone who has experienced both hallucinations and OOBEs will be able to distinguish quite clearly between the two. Most people who have had an OOBE and who have never read about them (or even heard much about them) have no difficulty in establishing in their own mind exactly what has happened to them. The experience is so real, so difficult to confuse with anything else, that they are convinced. People who have suffered hallucinations for whatever reasons –

illness, drugs, medication or mental illness – are often confused about what happened to them; about what they have seen or heard; about the 'realness' of the experience; about time or space within the experience. They often know that what they have experienced was an illusion brought on by their mental state – but they are not quite sure what it was that they went through. People who have had an OOBE do not often face this dilemma.

Other theories

There are some – coming from a Zen approach – who say we are always 'out' and that the feeling of an OOBE is merely a unique moment when we become aware of the fact. They say that nothing leaves the body to project or travel, as whatever it is is already out there having the experience continually. This theory works well until someone has an OOBE where they actually feel themselves 'leaving' and 'returning' – and then they *know* that they have been 'out' and 'returned'.

The other favoured theory is that an OOBE is nothing more than a psychosis of some kind. Unfortunately, this theory doesn't really clear up anything at all – it's a negative approach and doesn't seek to replace our current knowledge of OOBEs with anything better or more concrete. It is also insulting and unhelpful to people who have had such an experience. Telling someone that all they experienced was a mental aberration will cut no ice with them. It's a bit like Scrooge putting the ghost of Marley down to indigestion. It might explain things for a moment or two, but it doesn't really stand up to close inspection or parallel people's experience.

The Pentagon psychics

In the early 1970s, American intelligence experts set up a psychic research programme after being convinced that the Russians had a similar programme. Some officials in the Pentagon were certain that

the Russians would never be able to develop 'thought theft' by using psychics. Other officials, however, firmly believed that the Russians were likely to achieve a breakthrough and 'steal' the most important secrets that the Americans had. It was even believed that the Russians were on the verge of being able to enter the minds of senior officials and plunder them of their secrets.

A secret research facility was set up under the code name Project Scanate. It used volunteer members of the military who showed an aptitude for psychic ability. They were tested (at the Stanford Research Institute, Menlo Park, California) using various methods such as getting a recruit to 'guess' drawings being done several miles away, and were trained in a variety of psychic abilities, including astral projection, which was called remote viewing, as well as clairvoyance and precognition.

During the whole of the 1970s the research was conducted in an atmosphere of complete secrecy and other programmes were also set up along similar lines – Project Stargate, Grill Flame, Centre Lane and Sun Streak – and the first major test of the success they had achieved was in 1979 in the Iranian hostage crisis. The American military wanted to launch a rescue mission, but they couldn't find out where the hostages were being held. Pictures of the hostages were given to the recruits trained in remote viewing and they attempted to ascertain the exact location in Iran. Unfortunately, the precise success rate of their predictions wasn't known as the rescue plane crashed on its approach to Tehran.

Remote viewers were again used in 1986 to locate Colonel Gadaffi before the airstrike on Tripoli which failed to kill him, although a psychic did apparently locate him.

Since then, remote viewers have been used to 'spy' on a whole variety of situations. A remote viewer would be given a set of map co-ordinates and asked to 'visit' the site and to describe what he or she could see. The viewer would report back with vague impressions and the 'controller' would confirm if the viewer was on the right track.

Some remote viewers claim that they can explore every corner, room and corridor of a building and some claim that they can even go down elevator shafts.

The CIA is reported to be abandoning the research programmes as the success rates amounted to only about a 50 per cent 'hit rate', and that made it too unpredictable (other sources suggest it may be a budgeting problem, though). Chance or random guesses would have given them only a 20 per cent rate, so their extra 30 per cent seemed, as one official put it, 'to be a hell of a damned lot'. We have no information as to how far the Russians got with their research.

CASE HISTORIES

The case studies that follow have been drawn from a wide range of OOBEs. The people who have contributed their experiences have done so willingly and voluntarily.

JANE

I had come home from work quite early with a terrible migraine and I went straight to bed. The pain was intense, but I hadn't taken any tablets as they made me sick. I was lying on my bed in the darkness in my flat with my eyes closed, when I was suddenly aware that I was somehow hanging upside down. I opened my eyes and found myself looking straight down at myself lying on the bed. I figure I must have been up near the ceiling and upside down. It was really weird and I knew I should be really frightened, but somehow I wasn't. It was just like looking into a mirror. I wasn't aware of having any body or anything like that. I was just up under the ceiling looking down at me.

This went on for a few minutes, until I saw myself on the bed turning over. I couldn't feel anything at all. I was still but the other me, the real one, was moving. At that point I realised I couldn't feel my migraine and that was a blessed relief, but I also felt sorry for the other me as she seemed to be so uncomfortable lying on the bed. Then suddenly I was back in me on the bed feeling my migraine. I was lying on my side but hadn't felt myself roll over. I knew I had because I'd seen myself do it. It was really weird. As soon as I realised what had happened my headache vanished and

I got up. The whole thing worried me for a few days until my boyfriend said it was OK and that a lot of people had done the same thing. The strange thing is, I haven't ever had a migraine since; this was a couple of years ago, and I used to get them every few weeks.

Jamie

I'd been asleep and woke up in the early hours. I was aware that I was in my room and also not in my room – I was outside in the open air. Gradually I became more aware of being outside and less aware of being in my room. I realised I was standing on a hill near where we used to go on holiday when I was a kid. I felt I was sort of walking across the grass but not walking – sort of floating just above. There was someone coming towards me and he was also floating just above the ground. I recognised my father and he was smiling at me. It didn't seem at all strange that he'd died about five years ago. He was just there and wearing a really heavy tweed jacket and I remember thinking to myself that it didn't suit him – it was a horrid colour – a sort of orange.

He got up to me and we hugged. I remember the feel of this rough material of the jacket, which surprised me more than the fact that I was hugging my father. We'd never done that before. I'd never really got on with him and had left home very young – well, sort of run away really. I hadn't even gone to his funeral, and I guess I'd always felt a bit guilty about that. And here he was and it seemed quite right somehow. He patted me on the back and promptly vanished. I blinked, and when I opened my eyes I was back in my room, still in bed. Neither of us had spoken and I found myself crying.

The next day I went to see my mum who I hadn't seen since before Dad died. It was all a bit difficult, but we managed to talk a lot. I didn't tell her about seeing Dad – I don't think she'd of understood. She did tell me that I would have been proud of the way Dad looked when he'd been buried, as he'd been wearing his new tweed jacket. Apparently, Mum said, he'd been very proud of it, and I'd never seen it before he died. I wish I'd been closer to him, but feel somehow that he's forgiven me for giving him such a hard time before I left home. I'm glad I saw him again. The fact that it was all so strange never seemed strange at the time. I can remember how it all looked.

ERIC

When I was a child I used to look forward to going to bed as I liked
the floaty feelings I would get just before I went to sleep. I knew that
I was floating – usually just above my body. I liked the feeling and
assumed everyone did it before going to sleep. When I was older my
brother told me I was dreaming and that it didn't happen to anyone
at all. I heard about astral projection when I was in my mid-teens
and got a book about it. In the book it told you how to do it by
relaxing and visualising yourself out of your body. I never managed
to actually do that, but I did have one really powerful experience.
I'd been doing the relaxation techniques and I had my eyes closed.
I was lying on the bed when I suddenly felt myself being pulled
really fast down a long dark tunnel. The speed was faster than
anything I could ever imagine possible – literally millions of miles an
hour. As I went there seemed to be a sort of voice saying something.
Or rather it was telling me something important, but I can't quite
remember what it was. It was trying to tell me where I was or where
I was going and it sounded like 'You are now entering Cosmos
Seventeen'. But it wasn't quite that, only like that. It said it over and
over again as I went.

This journey went on for quite a while. Looking back I reckon it
must have been only minutes, but it seemed to last for an incredibly
long time. I was travelling head first and sort of lying face down but
my body, which I couldn't see as I still had my eyes closed, was sort
of fluid and flowing behind me. The sensation was like being made
out of water or mist. The tunnel had sharp bends and dips and my
body just seemed to curve round them as it followed my head.

At the end of the tunnel, I abruptly stopped and found myself at a
sort of cave mouth looking out over a vast plain. If you can imagine
a cave mouth half way up a cliff – that sort of thing – only the cliff
face was a million miles high and the plain was a million miles
wide. Filling the plain but not able to be seen – and I don't mean
invisible – just not letting itself be seen – was a vast something. I
don't know what it was, just that it was vast and I knew that it was
sort of round.

I stood there looking at this vast unseeable thing when I suddenly

became aware that it was very slowly but very deliberately beginning to turn around and that when it finally turned completely around it would look at me. Somehow I felt I had intruded and shouldn't be there – I wasn't worthy or ready or supposed to be there.

Then just as suddenly, and before the vast thing had completely turned, I found myself being sucked back down the tunnel.

The next thing I knew was that I was back in my bed. I was trembling all over and felt quite weak and cold. Whatever it was that I saw I don't know. I've never had another experience like it, but I've never forgotten it. Whatever it was I know I will have to go back one day and face it again, and I guess I try to live my life so that when it happens I will feel worthy enough. Don't ask me what that means, I don't know. But I do know that it influences me a lot. It wasn't scary, but it was truly awesome and I guess it haunts me a lot but not in a bad way. I don't like to put it into words too much, but if I was honest I guess I'd say I'd seen God, but luckily He didn't see me because I shouldn't have been there.

Beth

It seems really funny now, but it was pretty real at the time. I woke up and found myself standing next to the bed on my husband's side. I remember looking down and thinking how much I love him. Then I looked across and there was a woman in bed with him. I didn't stop to think about who she was or what she was doing there. It never occurred to me that I'd been in bed with him and that there couldn't be anyone else there with him. I flew round the bed in a dreadful rage and I mean 'flew'. It still didn't dawn on me that something bizarre was going on.

I got to the woman's side of the bed and tried to attack her. It's obvious now that it was no use. I couldn't hit her or pull her out of bed. Somehow my hands didn't work. They didn't go through her or anything like you see in films. They just didn't work properly. It was then that I realised that I was trying to attack myself. It was such a shock that I screamed. Then I woke up and I was myself again.

My husband laughed at me in the morning and said it was a dream,

but believe you me it was no dream. I know I was standing on his side of the bed and asleep next to him at the same time.

MARTIN

The only time it's ever happened to me was when I was a kid. I'd been invited to a party at some boy's house who lived quite a way away. I went to the party and don't remember much about it. Going home I got lost. I suppose I must have been about eight or nine at the time. I hated getting lost, still do, and I panicked completely. I was running and crying and trying to remember where I should have turned. The next thing, I was up above the roof tops looking down into the gardens. I could see myself running along and going in the wrong direction. I could even see the right way.

The next moment I was running along again. I turned around and found the right way to go. I never thought about it again until I was much older. It didn't occur to me that it was in any way unusual. I was running, then I was flying, then I was running again.

TREVOR

It was the middle of the afternoon on a winter's day and I was dozing in my chair in front of the fire. I thought I heard the door bell ring so I just got up to go and answer it. I got to the front door and didn't open it but just passed through it. There was no one there and I went back to the sitting room. I passed through the door and there I was still sitting in the chair. I remember thinking that it was the first time I'd ever seen me and I was a lot older than I thought. Then I was awake and sitting in my chair. I realised I'd passed through the sitting room door on the way to the front door and didn't even realise. Then the thought occurred to me that I hadn't realised at the time that I was out of my body. I think about it a lot, why it happened and everything, but I can't explain it.

ANDY

I was serving in the merchant navy during the war and my wife was living in London. I was really worried about her, what with all the

bombs and everything. I remember lying in my bunk, I think we were near Malta at the time, and the next thing I was looking down at our house in London. I don't know how I knew it was our house because I'd never seen it from up above, but I just knew. Then I was in our bedroom and my wife was asleep in bed and she seemed fine. She opened her eyes and said 'Hello, Andy, you on leave then?' and promptly went back to sleep.

The next thing I knew I was back in my bunk and I remember thinking how relieved I was that she was in bed alone. I guess that was the sort of thing we all worried about.

When I next went home my wife told me about this dream she's had where I suddenly arrived home on leave, and I told her what had happened to me. We used to laugh about it a lot and she said she could never be unfaithful to me because I could spy on her, although it never happened again.

Mary

I don't sleep well and never have done. I was lying awake early one morning when I found myself wandering through the house. I knew I was still in bed and yet I was also drifting slowly through the upstairs rooms. I looked in on all the children and they were all asleep. I saw the youngest, Peter, and he was half hanging out of bed with his arms on the floor. Then I was suddenly back in myself. I was so convinced that I'd been out of my body that I got up and went to Peter's room and he was exactly as I'd seen him. I've been able to do this several times since. I don't go far, only to the children's rooms to make sure they're sleeping. I always feel I could go anywhere when it happens, but forget to do so. Afterwards I think to myself I must try and go to my sister's house as she lives close by, but I never remember to do it when I'm doing it. I've never told anyone else about this as it seems silly, but I know I can do it. I can't always do it when I want to, but I can do it quite frequently.

Stephanie

I've been able to astral travel since I was very young. It happens quite often when I first start to drift off to sleep. I find myself floating

out of my body, usually coming out through my third eye. I like the feeling and float through walls looking at people asleep. I'm always amazed at how calm and detached I feel. I've never seen anyone else travelling while I've been. Sometimes I'm attached to my body by a thin cord that seems a bit like a rope and it seems alive. But often there's nothing there and I can go where I like. If I'm attached I don't seem to have as much freedom as when I'm not, but I don't know why there's a difference. I think that when I die it will be just the same as astral travel but permanently. I just hope there'll be more other people around or it might be a bit lonely for all eternity. I think everything has an astral double as you can sometimes see people sleeping and they have a sort of glow around them as if their astral body was just waiting to come out. I think it would be great to see my dog's astral body or to meet up with him when he's astral travelling. I'm sure that animals can do it because they've got souls like us.

Norman

(From his diary of time spent in the trenches during the First World War.)

Several hours of this misery passed and then an amazing change came over me, I became conscious, acutely conscious that I was outside myself, that the real 'me' – the ego, spirit or what you like – was entirely separate and outside my fleshy body. I was looking in a wholly detached and impersonal way upon the discomforts of a khaki-clad body, which, whilst I realised that it was my own, might easily have belonged to someone else for all the direct connection I seemed to have with it. I knew that my body must be feeling acutely cold and miserable but I, my spirit part, felt nothing.

Jill

But don't you think it's something everyone does as a child? I can remember going to bed and waiting to float upwards. I looked forward to it. You felt all warm and sleepy and then you knew you were going to go. You just floated upwards towards the ceiling. You didn't need to open your eyes or anything, you just floated. If you

felt suddenly excited about it or thought 'here I go' then it wouldn't happen; or if it had started to happen you'd find yourself back pretty quick. Sometimes you floated downwards – under the bed, I suppose. It was the same feeling you get in an elevator. That's pretty well the feeling, I suppose, just like being in an elevator. I haven't done it since I was much younger. I suppose it's something you just grow out of.

GORDON

I was staying at this house in Chelsea and it was one of those lazy, sunny, Sunday afternoons. We'd all eaten an enormous lunch and most of us were crashed out in the garden in deck-chairs or lying on rugs on the grass. It was one of those really magic days where there's a curious quality to sound, as if everything's hushed and unreal. Someone in the house put on a record – I remember it was a German band called Kraftwerk or something like that. The music was muffled and far away but seemed to vibrate up through the grass. I was just enjoying the sensation when I suddenly found myself inside the house going up the stairs. There were a couple of people coming down the stairs who I knew were also outside, I'd just seen them sitting near me. I looked at one of them and he just nodded at me in a sort of knowing way – as if he understood. I wandered about for a bit upstairs and then went downstairs again. I found myself looking out of the French windows at myself sitting in the deck-chair. The two people I'd seen on the stairs were standing near their own physical bodies. One of them suddenly swooped down into their body. I think at that point I blacked out or fainted with shock or something. Anyway the next thing I knew was I was waking up again in the deck-chair, although I don't think I'd been asleep for a single moment. The other couple were looking at me, but they didn't acknowledge that anything had happened and I didn't know how to talk about it, so I didn't. That was about twenty years ago and I have tried many times to repeat it. I've had some success, but it seems not to be something you can just do when you want to; there's some other rule to it that I just don't seem to be quite able to fathom . . . yet.

LESLEY

They began when I was about twelve and lasted for about two years, sometimes intensively and at others hardly at all. They stopped quite suddenly when I was eighteen and, apart from once or twice when I was first pregnant, they have never come back. And I can't say how relieved I am that they haven't. They always came at night as I was settling down to go to sleep. I tried everything – keeping the light on, playing the radio, keeping my eyes open, even praying – but nothing stopped them. I used to delay going to bed for as long as I could, I was so terrified.

I would lie there all screwed up with tension trying to sleep knowing it was going to happen. It wasn't like it was part of me – it was me. Suddenly I'd be up by the ceiling and the girl, the other me, would be lying on the bed below me. That's all it was and I don't know why it used to terrify me so much, but I could spend all day just dreading going to bed. And if I woke up in the morning without it happening it wasn't any better because then I knew it would happen that night without fail.

I can remember being up by the ceiling and then I would wake up and it was the next morning. I think the most terrifying part about it was that I didn't know anyone to talk to about it, and I was just frightened that I wouldn't be able to get back in. I thought that I would die up there, or rather the part of me left down there would die if I didn't go back, and as I didn't really understand what was happening or how to control it I didn't know how to go back. No, I wouldn't like to do it again, it scared me then and it still scares me now.

3

NEAR DEATH
EXPERIENCES

*A*s modern medical science has improved so dramatically in the past *few decades, and continues to do so at a phenomenal rate, it is hardly surprising that people who once would have gone beyond the point of being saved are now capable of being resuscitated from near death situations. As people increasingly are being 'brought back' from situations that only a few years ago would have proved fatal, it is no surprise to find an increasing number of accounts or reports of people's experience of such close encounters with death. It is certainly not uncommon to read newspaper reports of people who have nearly drowned or nearly been suffocated in avalanches or nearly been killed by a heart attack, and it seems quite frequently that the person involved often has an experience that goes beyond normal unconsciousness and often involves a sense of either leaving their body or being in some way consciously prepared for death. These experiences are quite rightly known as Near Death Experiences (NDEs).*

What is a NDE?

To be able to explore this fascinating subject we need to define, in some general way, what is meant by a NDE. Obviously someone who has crashed their car might say that they had a brush with death or if they were seriously ill they may say that they nearly died. But a true NDE involves something more. A NDE is usually defined

as having an actual experience of passing from life to death and somehow returning or being resuscitated. In Sabom's book *Recollections of Death* a NDE is defined as 'the experiential counterpart of the physiological transition to biological death'. That may be what a lot of people experience, but we need them to come back and tell us what happened; dying is not enough – we want to know what happens.

A typical NDE

From the many accounts of people who have nearly died and been resuscitated we can piece together a fairly general account of what happens and form a sort of corporate or general idea of the typical NDE. Obviously there will be many differences and a varied and wide range of descriptions. This is merely a typical account based on many accounts. There seem to be several recurrent themes that the majority of people experience.

- People who are seriously ill or injured are aware that they are in great pain and distress. They hear themselves being declared dead or identified as such. This seems to be an important trigger in many such experiences. They may hear a noise that is both unfamiliar and makes them feel uncomfortable. At the same moment they find themselves moving fairly rapidly down a tunnel of some sort. This tunnel either seems very dark or very light. Accounts vary but usually it is one or other of the two extremes; rarely is it vaguely dim or mildly light.
- They find themselves suddenly at the end of the tunnel and outside of their body. They can usually see their own body, often from above. They are aware of activity going on around their body; resuscitation attempts, medical staff. They frequently watch these proceedings with an air of disbelief which is rapidly replaced with emotional detachment – they are aware that they are dead and this realisation is usually accepted with a calm resignation.
- They are often aware that they still have a 'body' but it is markedly different from the one they have just left. While they watch the activity going on around their dead body they become aware that others have joined them – often 'spirit' forms of

friends and family long dead themselves. These visitors are greeted with the same air of detachment. The visitors often express or communicate in some way that they have been sent to help the recently deceased to 'cross over'.

- There is then the appearance or arrival in some way of a strange entity, often described as 'a being of light'. This being in a mysterious way shows the deceased their entire life; an instant playback of every event, every second that they have lived. This seems to be done not in a judgemental way, but merely to convince the deceased that they really are dead.

- The visitors and the being of light are usually described as 'full of love' or 'warm and loving'. The experience is nearly always pleasant. The visitors will often encourage the deceased to begin to move away from their abandoned physical body, and at this point the deceased often encounters some sort of barrier or non-visual wall which prevents them.

- If the 'being of light' has not been present, it will often appear at this point and communicate with the deceased and explain that they have to 'go back'. The deceased will often resist and want to stay outside of their body. There is often a message communicated that their time has not yet come, or that there is something they must go back and do.

- A moment later they find themselves back in their body. Sometimes they are conscious and sometimes not. If not, and they awake later, they remember the whole experience clearly and will often try to tell friends and family, but be unable to find the words to express the feelings that they had.

- Afterwards their views on life after death may well be radically altered and often there is a sense of extra life, a sort of gift, and of its being a bonus and not to be wasted.

What evidence is there?

Naturally there has been a considerable number of surveys done and research is currently being carried out. Psychologists have interviewed large numbers of people after they have 'died' and been resuscitated, and the figures indicate that around half would, to a

greater or lesser extent, fit in with our 'typical' NDE. Nearly all of those interviewed (about 95 per cent) said that the experience felt very 'real' and that they were aware that it was sufficiently different from a dream or a hallucination for them to be convinced that it was real. They said it was so vivid and 'believable' that it was often 'more real than real'. It felt as if something was properly 'real' for the first time in their life. They frequently reported the lack of suitable words to describe the feelings, and said that 'joy' and 'bliss' and 'love' and 'peace' were just not good enough to convey what they had experienced.

how common are NDEs?

As we saw earlier, medical science is 'calling back' more and more people. What was until recently considered fatal is now a situation from which someone can be 'resuscitated' with comparable ease. Surveys would indicate that about half of all people who have 'died' and then been revived have experienced something which could loosely be categorised as a NDE. Obviously the different stages reached vary enormously, but if some 50 per cent of people are experiencing something – and this covers the whole vast range of potentially fatal causes – then there is something happening, something leaving that can be experienced.

Something Leaving

A few years ago some experiments were carried out in which terminally ill patients were weighed at the point of death. Taking all possible factors into account, there was still an unexplained loss of body weight of around 39 grams (about the weight of an egg). These experiments took place in several countries independently of each other and all reached the same results. At the point of death the body suddenly and inexplicably weighs slightly less than it did seconds before.

Various theories have been put forward to explain what it is that leaves the body at death including: an 'astral' body that is

composed of some 'finer' material that is somehow 'invisible' under normal conditions; a burst of intense 'energy'; the soul; the spirit; 'some tangible aspect of self that can expand beyond the body'; an 'etheric' body; the physical manifestation of the personality; the accumulation of an entire life's thought-forms; the physical weight of consciousness; the ego; and the body's sensory input. Basically, we still don't know.

Where do the pyjamas come from?

This question was posed by the author C. J. Tart to ask how it is that when people have an OOBE or a NDE (or even a deliberate astral projection) their 'spirit double' is often clothed exactly as they were when they were in their physical body. Are the clothes manifested by thought? Is there an astral equivalent of their wardrobe? If we are capable of 'thinking up' our spirit clothes, are we not capable of 'thinking up' the whole experience? It would seem that the more a person knows previously about this subject the more they are likely to be wearing their pyjamas. Victims of sudden and unexpected accidents seem to have no similar notions – their body (if they have one at all) is often 'composed of light' or 'just a shiny globe of something that was me'. The pyjamas may not exist at all except in our imagination or our expectations.

Different stages of NDEs

Most of the people who have been interviewed have described something like the typical NDE I have just described, except that for many there were different 'stages' that they had reached. Some found themselves out of the body but went 'back' again before anyone else arrived. Others managed to get to the end of the tunnel before being whisked back. A few even managed to get beyond the barrier and found themselves in a beautiful landscape or caught a glimpse of another world. Research done so far seems never to have found anyone who encountered an experience that was not pleasant.

There may be reports of people being confused or in a state of emotional turmoil, but there seem to be no reports of anyone seeing anything frightening or 'hellish' or nasty.

However, some researchers suggest that anyone experiencing anything that indicated that life after death was in any way unpleasant or judgemental is likely either to not report it or forget it quite quickly – especially if the person concerned was aware that they'd not lived a 'good' life.

NDE tunnels

The tunnel seems to be seen by about half of the people experiencing a NDE and, of those, half see a tunnel of darkness and half see one of light. The dark tunnel has been described as a 'black vastness without shape or dimension, a void, a nothing – but a very peaceful nothingness'. The tunnel of light is usually described as 'golden and bright' or lit by the 'light of peace'.

About 10 per cent of people who have had a NDE managed to get as far as the 'other-world'. They all described it as beautiful or peaceful or somewhere very pleasant. The colours are often described as 'other-worldly' and there is often serene music playing.

Types of NDE

There seem to be two quite different NDEs, and they are not based on the person's religious life, beliefs or inclinations; nor on social attitudes, preconceived notions about life after death, or previous knowledge of similar accounts.

There are two types of people who have NDEs:

1 those who thought or knew in some way that they were going to die – known as perceived near death experience (PNDE);
2 those to whom it came as a shock – known as an unexpected near death experience (UNDE).

And the experience seems to be different for each type.

Perceived NDEs

PNDEs are usually experienced by the seriously ill or those undergoing prearranged surgery, and are frequently experienced by the elderly. A PNDE is often associated with the visitors and the journey to 'another world' as well as altered time perception and feelings of detachment. There is often another body to replace the physical body left behind. PNDEs usually have a more conscious return to their physical body.

Unexpected NDEs

UNDEs are usually experienced as the result of accidents, or by the victims of near fatal falls and drownings, electric shocks and car crashes. A UNDE is not usually associated with visitors or tunnels (light or otherwise), but is connected with the 'flashback' of one's life. There are often feelings of peace or happiness, and there is no subsequent body: 'I was just pure mind' is a phrase often used. UNDEs usually involve a sudden and unexpected return to the body.

Neither type of NDE mentions the classic 'silver cord' of traditional astral projection very often. This may be because it is 'absent' owing to the 'death' of the person, or that people who experience NDEs have heard, read or learnt little about such matters and thus are less inclined to have the type of experience that they may be 'expecting'.

What do such experiences teach us?

The one thing both types of NDE have in common is their ability to radically alter the experiencer's views about life after death. Various surveys have been carried out with people who have undergone NDEs and those who have been resuscitated without any such experience. Of those who experienced nothing of their near death, some 75 per cent said that they were just as afraid of death as they were before. Of the people who had experienced something of their near death which corresponded in some way to our 'typical' experience, some 90 per cent said that they were less afraid of dying than before and just over 80 per cent said that their belief in a life after death had increased dramatically.

The other fundamental changes that a NDE seems to produce are that the people resuscitated come back with a valuable 'lesson' that they believe they have learnt. This lesson is often associated with a profound and new 'love' – for other people, for life itself, for the wonders of the universe – a profound and unique love. The second change is that they have a new realisation about what is important in their life – a new opening up of their horizons. What is often reported is a fundamental shift away from pursuing goals of material possessions, 'getting on' and a new outlook of somehow 'being of some use'. Often they develop a new interest in helping others. It's as if their experience has opened their eyes to something bigger, something fundamentally more important than anything they'd ever considered before.

There is also evidence that a NDE subsequently promotes better mental health and improved social relationships; subjects feel more a part of humanity. Once they've had a glimpse of an 'after-life' there seems to be less worry about some of the 'trivia' of life that can weigh us down.

The three important changes which can then be characterised into a further definition of a NDE are:

- a loss or substantial lessening of fear of death
- a new and profound love for, and of, humanity
- a new awareness of one's horizons being wider than just one's self.

Obviously not everyone will be affected by these changes, but surveys indicate that as many as 75 per cent of people experiencing a 'typical' near death situation and subsequent resuscitation will be moved by such changes.

Obviously something significant is going on. But what? The possible 'scientific' explanations are of the usual negative sort – they explain away, but never explain. The physiologists' theories include cerebral anoxia and depersonalisation.

Cerebral anoxia

This explains NDEs as hallucinations due to oxygen starvation of

the brain. However, in many cases of near death and subsequent resuscitation there is simply no evidence that the brain has been starved of oxygen in any way. The people reporting NDEs are often well aware that what they have experienced is not a hallucination. Many of them have been seriously ill or extremely heavily medicated prior to their NDE, and have suffered or experienced hallucinations of the 'normal' sort quite often enough to be able to tell the difference. They have also often reported incidents or conversations that they could not possibly have been aware of if they were still physically resident in their bodies. Cerebral anoxia may explain some cases, but it certainly does not work as a blanket explanation for the majority of cases.

Depersonalisation

This theory, which is all to do with the way nature can numb us to extreme trauma, suggests that as the people have been resuscitated they were never 'clinically' dead. The fact that they have been 'brought back' shows, according to this theory, that the whole event has been some sort of personality disorder induced by their inability to face the reality that they were dying. However, there are sufficient numbers of reported cases where people were pronounced clinically dead and even more cases where people had no prior knowledge or warning that they were about to experience such an ordeal. There are a number of cases where people were unconscious at the time and would have had no time for their personality to construct such an elaborate scenario to explain away something that they themselves didn't even know they were undergoing.

Acceptance

Perhaps it's time simply to accept that what people experience, and what they believe they've experienced, can be accepted for what it is – a NDE. It may not be the complete picture, and obviously we won't get that and still be able to come back and tell. However, it is possible that we sometimes have a brief and significant glimpse of

what is to come. We can use this information to implement the three changes that seem to affect people who have gone through such an experience, without having to personally go through the trauma of a NDE ourselves.

flashbacks and life reviews

The flashback or life review which some NDEs have as part of their scenario are, according to the surveys, reported in about 25 per cent of all cases. However, in accident cases the figure is much higher – as high as 50 per cent according to some sources. People who report this phenomenon usually say that it takes place instantaneously – it's not like a movie where one scene follows another, but rather like a panoramic view of your life seen in its entirety in an instant. This playback is not done for anyone else's benefit – there's no judgement or sense of right or wrong. It's just an instantaneous recall for the benefit of the person experiencing it – more like a quick review to make sure nothing's been left unfinished or undone. Often when people have had the flashback and been resuscitated they will say that while the review was going on they were aware of how empty or shallow their life seemed. And it is this realisation that often returns them with a new-found sense of purpose – an attempt to make amends before it's too late.

There is nothing about 'doing good' in any of this – merely about 'doing something'. People realise that they have not looked about them, and they return seeking a wider perspective. They frequently undergo a personality reassessment where they deconstruct the old 'them' and replace it with a new more vital 'them' – one which has seen a larger picture and feels it has something of value to offer.

More alive than alive

One aspect of a NDE often reported is that while they were 'dead', people felt more alive than when they were alive. This feeling of 'more alive than alive' is often an explanation of their new-found vitality and sense of purpose when they return. They sometimes say

that they have been made aware that they weren't really living before, and they are trying to inject a sense of being more alive into the remainder of their life – they've had a 'wake-up' call.

If these experiences of near death can have such a poignant and deep-seated effect then there is every reason to accept them in their entirety – time wasted trying to disprove or discount them both undervalues the people who have had the experience and dismisses the benefit of the experience itself. If we accept the reality of the experiences and their benefits for those concerned, we can learn a lot from them and use that information to improve and refine our own views on death and our survival beyond that death.

The International Association for Near-Death Studies (IANDS)

IANDS was set up in London (see 'Useful information' for their address) by a group of doctors and scientists who were interested in researching the subject of NDEs further. They collect and evaluate case studies and they also try to assess the significance of the experiences to those who have undergone them. As we saw earlier in this chapter, the effects can be dramatic and beneficial and, as such, may be a valuable aid to learning more about how people can become positive in their outlook on life and less afraid or apprehensive about what happens to them after they have died.

The Natural Death Centre (NDC)

The NDC was originally set up to research into alternatives to euthanasia but has now expanded to include courses and seminars

on death, bereavement and grief counselling. It is run by a team of psychologists who also research and collect accounts of NDEs and are especially concerned with 'dignified' death. They can also help people draw up 'living wills' which would allow a person's relatives to stop treatment if he or she is suffering from a long-term fatal illness and the relatives consider that the person has arrived at a point where further treatment would only prolong the misery.

The NDC also investigates all aspects of 'dignified' dying, including alternative funeral services, reusable coffins, 'green' funerals, memorial planting of trees, and DIY coffins. (See 'Useful information' for their address.)

CASE HISTORIES

David

We were all in Greece on a boat my father had chartered. I guess I was about ten and my brother twelve. I fell overboard. I remember looking up through the clear water and seeing the shape of the boat clearly. I remember the boat was painted a vivid blue underneath which I'd not seen before. Then suddenly I was standing on the deck watching my father and brother pulling this boy up out of the water. He looked pale and, although I could see my father's mouth moving, I couldn't hear anything. It was only later that I realised the boy was me. It didn't seem unusual or anything – one minute I was in the water and the next I was on deck watching. Then I saw my father's mother standing at the far end of the boat watching me watching them. That was strange because she'd died the year before. She smiled at me and beckoned me to her. I went over to her and she put her arm round me and hugged me. Then she pushed me away from her and back towards my father. He was giving the boy the 'kiss-of-life'. I looked back at my grandmother and she sort of nodded at me as if I was expected to do something. I didn't know what. The next thing I was lying on the deck being sick and my brother was crying. I realised I could hear again. I tried to tell my father all about it later, but all he said was I had to wear a life-jacket.

I've never told anyone else, but I'm certain I was dead for a moment or two. It's certainly been useful to me because I know that I will have something of the same sort of experience when I die. I guess I'm not afraid of dying, although I must admit I don't think about it much.

GEORGE

My mother was in the hospital in Birmingham dying of cancer. She'd been given a fortnight to live, which was very accurate because she did die exactly two weeks after being admitted. I went to see her every day and she was brilliant. She knew she was dying and said it was all right because she was very tired and her body wasn't working as well as it used to. I think she was ready. About a week before she died she asked me to take her outside to get some fresh air and I wheeled her in her wheelchair out into the garden. It was a very warm day and we sat and chatted for a while and she fell asleep. But it wasn't just a sleep. Her breathing became very slow and there was a 'death-rattle' to it, if you know what I mean. Her mouth fell open and I was sure she was about to die. It seemed a really good time for her to go. There were flowers all around her and she'd been peaceful. I sat watching her and sort of urging her to go on. I didn't say anything, I was just mentally willing her to get it over and done with. Her breathing got slower and slower until it stopped altogether for a few moments. She looked very peaceful and I remember thinking how much I loved her and how happy I was that it was all so easy for her.

Then suddenly she sat up and demanded to be taken back inside. She seemed angry and upset. I wheeled her back in and she asked me to go – well, she told me to in no uncertain terms actually.

I went back that evening and she was in a better mood. We had a cup of tea together and she apologised for being so rude. She said that when she was sleeping she was suddenly aware that the garden was full of people and that Pop (my grandfather) was there (he died nearly twenty years ago). My mother said that some of these people had been stroking her hair and that they were all lovely. But she said that she then started arguing with them as they were trying to get her to go with them and she was damned if she was going then.

She wasn't going until my brother had been to see her and he was on his way back from the States. She'd not been angry with me, but with these 'other people' because they'd seemed so insistent and she told them she still had a week left and was going to have it 'come hell or high water'. Which she did. I wasn't there when she died and I regret that, but it was in the early hours of the morning and I'm sure it was fine for her. It is nice to know she wasn't going to be lonely, and I quite look forward to seeing Pop again myself, one day.

Billy

Well it certainly sorted me out. Before I don't think I was very nice to know at all. I've tried hard to be a lot better since. I guess I smoked too much and I know I drank far too much. I was overweight and seriously unfit. What happened was that I came home fairly tanked up one night. Everyone was in bed so I was trying not to make any noise. My wife said later that she'd heard me come in – you know how drunks think they're trying to be quiet when they're waking up the whole household. I remember sitting on the toilet and the next thing I knew was that I was standing above myself looking down and I had collapsed on to the floor. My wife said she heard the crash and knew something serious was going on. I'd had a fairly major heart attack. I saw her come running into the bathroom and try to turn me over on to my back. I remember thinking at the time that there was no point – I was dead and that was all there was to it. I looked around to wander off as I felt so calm, so uninvolved with this dead body on the floor – or even my wife and children come to that – that I was ready to just go on to whatever it was that I was supposed to do next.

The next thing I knew was I was rushing headfirst down this tunnel for a very long time. It was very dark and long, and then I was awake the next morning in the hospital. I wasn't particularly happy to be back, I can tell you. I realised then I had to do something about myself if I was going to have to continue living. I don't remember having a 'body' when I was looking down at myself, but I wasn't happy to be back in the fat one I woke up in. I've given up drinking, lost a lot of weight and I have even taking up riding a bike

again to get fit. I haven't quite managed to cut out smoking all together but I'm trying my best. My wife says I'm a different person since. I feel the same but a lot more positive. I now know that there's some sort of life afterwards.

JOANNE

I hadn't been a nurse very long when I had to attend my first death. I was on night duty and a little girl had been brought in who had been diagnosed as having leukaemia some months previously. She was very quiet, very ill, and the chemotherapy had caused her to lose all her hair so she looked so tiny. She was sick in the night and slipping in and out of consciousness all the time. Her parents were with her and we were trying to make her as comfortable as possible. The last time she came round she said she was going soon, that 'they' had arrived and she was going to play with them. She said there were beautiful lights all around her. Then she slipped away. She was smiling as she died and all the pain had left her poor little face. I was upset but I felt that she was going somewhere nice. I haven't been so worried about death since then. If they came and looked after that little girl perhaps they'll look after me as well when I die.

CHRISSIE

I was working in a deli in New York in the sixties when this guy comes in late one night and starts sounding off at us. He was a maniac of some kind and shouting about the aliens were coming. I turned to call the cops when I felt this kinda dull ache in my back and I fell down. I lay there and Marcia was screaming that I'd been stabbed. I didn't feel stabbed, just sore and uncomfortable. I remember watching as the mad guy was still running around with the knife. The cops came and an ambulance and I watched myself being worked on by the paramedics. I don't know how I was watching myself, but I was. I was sort of hovering around. I knew I was badly injured but I certainly didn't think I was dead until one of the paramedics said 'We've lost her'. Then I knew and it felt fine. I was curious to know what they were doing to me and I remember being quite annoyed that I couldn't see because they were crouched over me. Then I opened my eyes and I was looking at the

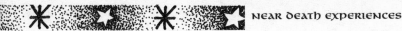

floorboards from real close up and I knew I was back. I got taken to the hospital in the ambulance and the same thing happened on the way. One minute I was lying there with these two guys doing things to me and the next I was way up above the ambulance looking down on it. I wasn't bothered when I saw it driving away. I knew it had my body in it and that I was dead, but it didn't seem important. So what, I thought. I was quite surprised that I'd been stabbed to death at work; I thought I'd die a little old lady somewhere. Then I was suddenly back in my body and I was in the hospital, so maybe I will die a little old lady after all. I was quite pleased not to have been stabbed to death as I think it's not a nice way to go.

Su Lee

I was passenger in car which crashed. I was thrown through window and landed in road. Everything went black and I was falling down a long way. I thought I must be going to hell as I'd been a silly girl before, always being wild. Then it was all light and I think I in Heaven. It was nice with angels and everything. I wanted to stay but they said I had to go back. I woke up in hospital and doctors say I died but they win me back from death's door. Since then I not so wild any more and I now training to be a healer. I want to help everybody so much now. I still got some scars on my head, but not much now.

Stan

I knew it was going to happen. I'd had this dream and I'd seen my bike turning over and over in the air in slow motion. I could have gone to work in the car but it was a nice day and quite sunny. It was May the first so it was a sort of mayday for me all right. All the way to work, and it's about twenty miles, I kept looking at cars and thinking 'That's the one that's going to get me' and I was riding quite slowly to avoid everything. As I got into Bristol there's a steepish hill and I was behind a lorry which suddenly turned left with no warning, just as I was about to overtake it. I managed to brake and miss it, and I thought as I watched it turn that I was lucky. I thought that it was the lorry that was destined to get me and somehow I'd escaped. I opened the bike up and just as I did so another truck pulled

out from the turning. I'd not seen it as the first lorry was blocking my vision. I hit the second lorry head on and the next thing I knew, I was flying through the air. Only it wasn't me. Well, it was me but I was really flying. I could look down and see tiny cars and houses below and I knew I was a goner. It was great. I've always wanted to fly and I was. It felt really free. Then I was back on the ground lying face down with a mouthful of tarmac and an ambulance man standing over me. I said 'Tell me I'm going to be all right', and he said 'I think so'. Then I was out again and flying. I stayed out for quite a while I think because I came round again in the ambulance. I was in hospital for six weeks and I certainly had plenty of time to think about it all. I gave up bikes after that, but I'm learning to hang-glide now. It's not the same, but it's the nearest thing I can get to the feeling of flying I had.

Alistair (first NDE)

Travelling back in separate vehicles with a friend from collecting building materials – country lanes – blossoming hedgerows, and a sense of elation brought on by satisfaction and contentment; the appearance of warm bright sunshine after a shower. Happy music on the car radio; windows wound down; speed winding up. Suddenly vision of somewhere close by and a clear view of my car skidding into an oncoming vehicle; feeling I should slow down. Slow down due to strength of what I saw; round bend to come head-on with a tractor – no room to pass. I press the brake hard and glide straight into the front of the tractor with the constant knowledge that I'm going to be OK because I slowed down. Not hurt at all; strange and strong feeling of elation at the vision; no concern for the car or anything – a desire to feel and look normal, so show slight annoyance at the state of my car but really I don't care – no shock as no surprise.

Finally on returning home some four hours later my friend immediately asks me if I had a car accident with the tractor as, when he passed it only minutes before me he had a strong feeling that I would not make it past.

Ensuing days filled with massive elation due to a feeling of insight and privilege due to having been in a state that caused a connection to be made in the fabric of time.

TERRY

During the war I saw a lot of men die, but seeing Jimmy was the worst. We got dropped behind enemy lines in France and they knew we were coming. Someone had tipped them off and they were waiting. I got down OK and stowed my chute, but Jimmy caught it as soon as his feet touched the ground. I think it must have been a mortar, the bloody mess it made of him. There wasn't two bits you could have put back together. We had no time to do anything for anyone and just made for the trees. It was fairly dark and I was running low when I was suddenly shocked to see Jimmy running alongside of me. The bloody fool was dead and didn't even know it. I shouted at him to get out of it but he just kept up with me. Then he suddenly stopped and ran his hands through his hair. Then he looked at me and winked. I think that was the most shocking thing I saw throughout the whole war – that wink. Oh, he knew he was dead all right, he was just playing with me for a moment before going on. Bloody fool thought it was funny being dead, and it suddenly made the whole damned war seem pointless. What's the point if you're trying to stay alive and kill the other fellow when it's just a joke? I ask you, what's the bloody point?

KENTON

My girlfriend had invited me round to supper and she'd cooked seafood pasta which I don't really like. My stomach had been playing up all day so I couldn't eat much and I think she was a bit put out. Then I got these really sharp pains and she thought I was messing about, sort of teasing her, but I wasn't. The pain got really bad and Cathy said she'd take me to the hospital, but I said that all I needed was some aspirin or something. She said that the hospital would have some, clever girl, because she knew I'd never agree to go. When we got to the hospital I don't remember much about it as I was pretty delirious by then, but I do remember being in a room of some sort and being sick in a sink but there was nothing to chuck up. There was this stream of green and yellow light coming out of my mouth but it wasn't streaming away from me, I was streaming away from it. The sink got further away until everything was like

looking down the wrong bit of a telescope, really very far away and small. I remember thinking that this yellow and green light was my life pouring away but I couldn't work out how; if it was my life how come I was still thinking? None of it made sense. I remember looking down at the room with this sort of telescope vision and I could see me holding on to the sink with both hands. Then it all got so far away that I couldn't see anything except a tiny dot of light, and I remember thinking it was like turning the television off when I was a kid, you got this tiny white dot which lasted for a while before the screen went black. I thought 'That's it then, the telly of my life's just switched off'. Then I heard this voice and it was the sort of voice you'd expect some hammy actor to have if he was playing God, sort of all deep and grammar schoolish, and it said 'Game over'. I remember I did this sort of silent scream and shouted a couple of swear words. Not because I believed I was dead or anything; it was just that I felt Cathy and me hadn't been given a chance. Then this voice says 'Oh, all right then, game on again'. Then I woke up the next day with my appendix taken out. Apparently it had burst just as they had operated but I wasn't ever really in any danger. I don't know if this was the sort of thing you mean by a near death experience, but it certainly opened my eyes. I married Cathy. I don't eat seafood pasta and I think I was dead for a little bit. That's all.

Adrian

I must have been only four or five and we were living in Leeds. I don't remember the house, but my mother said it was on the side of a hill so that the back was much taller than the front. I fell out of an upstairs window. I had been standing up looking out when it had just opened. I didn't touch anything. I don't remember falling but I do remember hitting the ground. I landed on my chest and it knocked all the air out of me. There was this lady there and she said she would look after me. I held her hand and we waited for my mother to come. When she did she ran straight past us to this pile of clothes on the ground and picked them up. I realised then it was me she was picking up but I was still holding this nice lady's hand. She then said I could go back now and I was in my mother's arms

screaming my head off. I had to stay in the hospital for one night. There was nothing wrong with me apart from a couple of scratches and I couldn't see properly for a day or two, everything was blurry.

James

I had been potholing in a place called Swildon's Hole which is near Wookey in Somerset. We'd made it down to Sump 1, which is quite an easy climb down, and Swildon's was quite dry, which makes it easier. Sometimes the river flows through at such a rate you get exhausted before you've gone five yards. But it was an easy climb down. Sump 1 is the first deep pool. You can dive through if you hold on to the rope that goes under and you come up the other side. I was wearing a wet suit and had made the dive several times before. It's cold and dark, but as long as you keep hold of the rope and keep swimming you're all right. It's about as far as you can swim holding your breath and you have to really pull yourself along with the rope for the last bit. I guess I was about halfway when I lost the rope. I reached about for it a bit but couldn't find it again. You can't come up for air as the pool is a sump with the rock under the water that you're going under. I panicked and sucked in a lot of water.

It's pitch black in there and suddenly it wasn't. There was this amazing light and I felt as light as a feather. I couldn't feel the cold any more. I couldn't feel anything. Then the light, which had been about as bright as anything I thought could be, got even brighter. I can't really explain it but the light was alive. It was living light and it was full. I don't know what it was full of. I would say love, but that sounds stupid and nothing like what it was. There was this noise too, bit like sonic booms. I don't know how I felt – big enough to fill the universe and at the same time as small as anything. And I felt really important, like this light was really pleased to see me, like I was part of it or something. Then this light was pushing me away and I was really crying because I didn't want to go away from it. It was the best thing I've ever felt – sort of like the best feelings you've ever had in your life, times ten million.

That was the last thing I remembered until I came round outside of Swildon's. My mate had dived in and dragged me out and another

party of potholers had carried me unconscious all the way back. I don't know how they passed me along because it's pretty narrow in places but I guess I must've been pretty limp. Anyway if dying is anything like going back to that light, I'd be happy to go now.

Alistair (second NDE)

Go out with two friends to buy four-wheel-drive. Take if off road, into field. Sudden feeling of foreboding but dismiss warning signals. Driver loses control of vehicle, which slides down steep bank and head-on into six-foot ditch. I was not driving and had no control. Complete sense of disempowerment. Very heavy impact and myself and female friend narrowly miss going through windscreen – sustain bad minor injuries.

In silence of aftermath big feeling by all three of us that we should not have got off so lightly considering the conditions. When leaving scene notice dog-fox watching us close by the middle of field – walks quietly away – no rush.

We do not encounter anyone for at least an hour after the accident due to remoteness, and a bigger sense of detachment comes on.

Following four/five days consumed with a sensation of having left my soul in the vehicle, as if one of my lives had been extinguished there and that I was only a ghost of my real self. A childish feeling of not having heeded my instinctive warnings clouds my everyday vision.

Still cannot find a physical reason as to why we managed to come away from an accident (no seat-belts) that to all intents and purposes should have been fatal.

CHAPTER 4

PRACTICAL TECHNIQUES OF ASTRAL PROJECTION

Traditionally there were many techniques offered as being valuable to anyone wanting to try astrally projecting themselves. Often these techniques were dressed up in esoteric or magical ritual. They were even denied to a wide cross-section of people on the grounds that the techniques should be 'secret' or that they should form part of some arcane lore that was to be made available only to people who had gone through some rigorous and bizarre apprenticeship or initiation ceremony or ritual.

However, the evidence seems to prove that the traditional view is just nonsense. The techniques require no training beyond themselves; they are not secret; they are not dangerous; they belong to no-one in particular; they have no magical or 'power' abilities; and they certainly are not difficult or capable of being learnt only by some (usually self-appointed) élite. They are simple, easy and safe. They can be learnt by anyone and they most certainly can be practised by anyone.

There does seem to be a certain 'type' of person who achieves a greater success at astral projection than others. Usually, though not always, these people are what you might call 'creative' or 'imaginative'. They are the sort of people who can get lost in a book or a computer game or film; the sort of people who can daydream for hours; the sort of people who have to be called several times before they'll take notice if they're engrossed in some project. Arthur O'Shaughnessy summed them up best in his poem simply called *Ode*:

> *We are the music-makers,*
> *And we are the dreamers of dreams,*
> *Wandering by lone sea-breakers,*
> *And sitting by desolate streams;*
> *World-losers and world-forsakers,*
> *On whom the pale moon gleams;*
> *Yet we are the movers and shakers*
> *Of the world for ever, it seems.*

Is this you? It may not matter if it's not, it's just that the dreamers, the creative types, are the ones who, on average, seem to do better when they try to learn how to project themselves. However, there are many cases of sensible, down-to-earth folk having just as good results. All you can do is try it and see how you get on. Mind you, you probably wouldn't be reading this far if you weren't fairly imaginative, creative and open to new ideas.

Hints and tips

Obviously astral projection requires a degree of dedication: it's not a subject that can be treated too lightly. You may well have to practise many times before you have any degree of success and you can't just give up after five minutes if you want to achieve a result. There are also some conditions that you should try to avoid prior to practising. They are:

- **anger or irritation** – you need to be calm and relaxed;
- **stress** – you need to be relaxed and at ease, so avoid trying to practise when you are worrying about something;
- **excess food or drink** – you should not try to practise on a heavy or over-full stomach;
- **extremes of temperature** – being too warm or too cold;
- **extremes of emotion** – obviously you won't want to try to practise if you are feeling particularly miserable, but you should also avoid trying when you are elated or over-excited;
- **extremes of mental awareness** – being too tired or too wide awake;

- **uncertainty within yourself** – it seems that people who are 'balanced' have a better chance of success. Astral projection is not a therapy – it may give you answers about how consciousness can exist outside of the body, but it will not solve your problems;
- **lack of emotional harmony** – being in a secure and loving relationship seems to indicate a better chance of success, although others shouldn't be put off by this. It's when your relationship is going through a crisis that a lack of success seems inevitable;
- **lack of a support system** – you need to be able to talk to the people around you about astral projection and receive their support. If you feel it is somehow wacky or wrong, or you are in any way 'doubtful' about it perhaps you need to question your approach. Evidence seems to indicate that those people who have an open and honest attitude to astral projection achieve a better than average success rate;
- **lack of a belief system** – those who have a belief system (and it doesn't seem to matter what – anything from Tantric Buddhism to Catholicism) seem to achieve better results. People who are 'seekers', looking for a belief system, seem to produce less successful results;
- **using astral projection for the 'wrong' reasons** – trying to use astral projection to 'spy' on people or somehow gain power over others or any similar purpose just doesn't work. The beauty of astral projection is that once you're 'out' you cease to be governed by physical trivialities, and you can't get 'out' until you abandon them anyway.

So, those are the basic guidelines. However, there are actually no rules with astral projection. These are hints and tips based on other people's experience and they may not fit yours at all. Only by practising will you discover what is right for you.

GETTING BACK IN

The majority of people who have consciously projected say that you can return as quickly as you want to merely by *willing* yourself back in. Also any situation you encounter – such as a strange noise or

light or wind – will immediately take you straight back in. There is absolutely no evidence that you can get 'stuck' out, or be attacked, or get lost and not be able to find your physical body again, or go too far, or be 'taken over', or any of the many other horror stories you might have heard.

ÐRUGS

There are many cases where people have attempted to astrally project by using drugs of one sort or another (usually hallucinogenic drugs). I seriously **would not** recommend this. There have been too many cases of 'acid psychosis' where the drug user ends up either believing the hallucinogenic experience to be 'real' or being unable to 'control' the experience or, even worse, having the hallucinogenic experience on a permanent or semi-permanent basis. There are also cases of 'flashback' where the drug user has recurring hallucinations without taking any subsequent drugs.

There simply is no getting away from the fact that **using drugs can seriously damage your mental, emotional and spiritual health**. Don't do it.

CAUTIONS

Ðuality

Let's suppose you have had a measure of success and have managed to get 'out'. What can go wrong? Well, actually very little. However, there are a few situations where you may become confused, disorientated or apprehensive. The main cause of these conditions will be a state known as *duality*. This is where you are out and can 'see' your physical body and at the same time you are aware of also being in your physical body and seeing the other you. At this moment your consciousness will seem to be in both places at once. The first time it happens can be extremely disconcerting – a form of temporary mild schizophrenia may ensue. The best advice is to

either return at once to your physical body (best done by simply 'willing' yourself back) or to get your 'out' self to turn away and not look at the physical you. The seat of consciousness should then go with the astral 'you', and the physical 'you' will lose awareness of the other you. Another tip is to project only with your eyes closed if you encounter this problem with any frequency.

Multiple bodies

Sometimes (but rarely) encountered is the multiple bodies situation where you are 'out' and are aware that there may be more than one of 'you' out. This one seems to be merely a strange illusion and the seat of consciousness (as far as we know) is with only one of the 'out' bodies – the one that is you.

Paralysis

Often just before or upon returning you will have a feeling that your physical body is paralysed in some way. For a moment or two you may panic. You don't need to – the paralysis is quite normal and will disappear quickly. Stay still until feeling returns to your body and you can carry on as before. This state of paralysis is known as a cataleptic or, sometimes, catatonic state and is frequently encountered. Some people never experience it and others do every time they project.

Psychic wind

Sometimes, when you are out, you will encounter a strange wind. It can blow quite fiercely or relatively softly and will spring suddenly from nowhere. If you are in an enclosed room and you know that there can be no wind it can be quite disconcerting. However, this wind can do you no harm. Many explanations have been given for it including solar energy, but no one really knows for sure what it is. It's traditionally been known as psychic wind.

Astral noises

You may sometimes hear strange noises: loud bangs, sonic booms,

high-pitched whistles. These unexplained phenomena may disconcert you but they cannot harm you. Some of them can be extremely pleasant and were known traditionally as the music of the celestial spheres, or the harmony of the heavens. One quite common noise has been described as 'someone playing a one-note flute in a forest of wind a long way away'.

The worst the noises can do is make you jump – sometimes quite literally back into your skin.

Astral sex

Some people who have consciously projected have reported that while they were 'out' they have met other astral bodies of the opposite sex, and claim that they have had sex with them on the 'astral plane'. These reports cannot be disproved or confirmed and often they fit into the 'friend of a friend' category of story. I would be more than happy to collect any case studies of your own, if you have them.

Long distance travel

Some people claim to be able to project vast distances and even visit other planets or solar systems. The current advice is to stay near your body and don't overdo things to begin with.

Fear

A common phenomenon that presents itself to people who are just learning to meditate is that they will see 'faces'. These faces are often described as 'devilish' or like 'demons'. They can be quite easily explained: when you stare into a dark space for any length of time your mind will try to make 'patterns' out of the blackness. The most common such pattern for humans is the one thing we can identify most easily – the human face. For people experienced in meditation these faces disappear of their own accord and usually quite quickly – they are just a phase you go through.

Astral projection has similar phases. While 'out' you may 'see' or think you see such faces. They are merely your consciousness trying to make some sense of what is basically an abnormal or new situation. Remember that nothing can harm you and you will be fine. These 'apparitions' will vanish once you tell yourself that they are nothing more than your own mind being silly and playing with you. The ego doesn't like to be undermined, and anything that shows you what a shallow beast the ego really is – like meditating or astral projection – is a threat. Your ego may well play tricks on you at first to get you to stop. The ego likes to be in control and anything you do to usurp its power will not be entertained lightly. However, the ego can be reassured quite easily and all you have to do is say to yourself: 'It's OK, I'll be back in a moment' and the ego, like a deserted puppy, will settle down to nap while you are away. You may get an excited greeting when you return.

Ethics

Difficult one this. We all have our own rules and standards of behaviour and, as long as it affects or harms no-one else, there's not much that's 'forbidden'. However, astral projection seems to 'push buttons', especially amongst the deeply religious. You may well be told it's 'wrong' or even 'evil'. I'm afraid that this is something you will have to deal with yourself – only you can know how you feel about such things. The suppression of knowledge may be more wrong.

DISCLAIMER

As we, the author and publishers, cannot have any control over the situation and circumstances under which you may practise astral projection, we cannot be held liable for any ill effects.

You should be a responsible adult, acting of your own volition, and in sound mental, emotional, spiritual and physical health. If you are not then please do not attempt any of the following techniques.

Ideal conditions

Like the hints and tips we covered earlier in this chapter these are 'average' ideal conditions under which the most successful projections have been found to happen. If anything here appears to contradict the instructions given for individual techniques described later, simply follow those specific instructions.

- **A suitable place** – You need a quiet room and one where you will not be disturbed. You will not be able to relax if you think someone could come in at any moment. This is where you need the support of friends and family – you need to be able to explain what you are doing and have your space inviolate for the time you are using it to project. Failing that, lock the door. The room you choose should be one in which you feel comfortable, safe and 'at home'. If you share your bed with someone else and want to trying projecting as you lie alongside of them (or with them if they share your enthusiasm), then perhaps you and your partner need to work out some prearranged code for when you don't want to be disturbed – a single squeeze of the hand means 'I'm off now, see you up there', or something like that.
- **Quiet** – It's important that telephones, door bells, children shouting, visitors and other loud disturbances are either eliminated (if possible) or reduced to a barely noticed minimum. If you can't get enough quiet you could always tune a radio to 'white noise' (or not tune it) to blank out background sound. Music is not really a good idea (unless you are using *Technique 19 – Audio/visual aids*).
- **Comfort** – If you are lying down you need firm support from your bed. You need to be neither too warm nor too cold. Your body temperature will drop while you are projecting so you need to be able to cover yourself in a blanket or something when you return – you'll feel colder when you come back.
- **Clothing** – You should wear loose, comfortable clothing. You don't have to dress up, nor do you have to be nude. Remove all jewellery, spectacles, contact lenses (you'll be able to see fine when 'out'), watches, wigs, and false limbs and teeth.

- **Lighting** – Total darkness can be too intense, and full light can be a distraction. You need dim lighting – a soft glow is good – enough to be able to see but not too bright or dark.
- **Atmosphere** – Some people like to light incense or 'prepare' in some way. This is fine, but not really essential. The one thing you need to avoid is anything that is liable to distract you – worrying that the joss stick might have fallen over and be setting light to the room is a distraction.
- **Time of day** – If you try to project only last thing at night, just before you go to sleep, you'll be tired. What you need then is sleep, not projecting. The best results happen when you are not too tired nor too wide awake. You need to be relaxed but not sleepy. Try going to bed, to project, a little earlier than you would normally go. You shouldn't be too tired then. A good time is upon first waking in the morning – you'll be in the right place and at the right time.
- **Body movements** – You may find a reaction to projecting similar to that found by some people new to meditating – they are unable to keep still for more than a moment or two. They find that if they are just relaxing they don't have this problem, but as soon as they start trying to meditate their bodies suddenly develop a need to wriggle, itch, twitch, get up to go to the bathroom, feel uncomfortable, get cold, yawn, sneeze, blink a lot, go to the bathroom again, suddenly remember something important that has to be done, forget what they're supposed to be doing and generally be quite difficult and unresponsive. Projectors experience the same things – it's that old ego again. If you persevere you'll find that all these irritations will vanish. You can give into them for a bit, but if you ignore them they will disappear. If you feel a need to swallow because your mouth has filled with saliva, then swallow. Likewise if you need to scratch or blink, do it. It's when the physical sensations of discomfort become unbearable that you need to ignore them.

The techniques

Technique 1 – Relaxation

Follow all the ideal conditions listed above. Lie down on your back with your arms by your side. Your head should be level and not raised up. Some people prefer to dispense with their pillow altogether and one projector said that he achieved great results by just lying on the floor in the yoga 'corpse' position. This is where you lie down with your arms by your side and legs straight. It is recommended by some 'experts' that you align yourself along a north–south axis with your head in the north position. Again you will have to experiment with this and see what works best for you.

Some successful projectors recommend that you cross your arms over your chest with your palms face down. Others suggest that your legs should be crossed at the ankles. Again try all these different positions until you find one that works for you.

Once you are comfortable you can close your eyes and begin to relax completely. The best way to do this is to start with your feet and slowly, mentally, work your way up the body imagining each part being completely relaxed.

You'll end up at the top of your head but don't stop there. Imagine the space just outside of your head also relaxing. Then imagine your consciousness beginning to fill that relaxed space.

This technique is best left to a 'try it and see' approach. What happens while you're lying there will be different each time. The important thing seems to be to get into a completely relaxed state – so relaxed that you can't even feel your body. This may be the perfect requisite for entering the classic cataleptic trance state so highly thought of by traditional writers on astral projection.

Sometimes you may feel your consciousness begin to leak out from the top of your head. The first thing you'll do, if you're like everyone else, is to get excited. And the next thing is you'll be back in your

body so fast you'll wonder if you didn't imagine it all. The problem with projecting is that your respiration and heart rate needs to be slow and constant. The second you feel that first 'lift' of your consciousness you immediately think 'Here I go', and the heart speeds up, as does your breathing. Then you're back and having to start all over again.

The only cure for this 'catch-22' is to train yourself not to be goal-oriented. Learn not to care whether you feel anything or not. Pretend to yourself that you're doing some yoga or practising a stress management technique, and whatever you do, don't concentrate on projecting.

By letting whatever happens just happen, you'll achieve a better degree of success. If you are too focused on projecting you'll have too much at stake and this makes you elated when it begins to happen – then it stops happening. The trick is exactly that – a trick. You trick yourself into being calm about the whole thing.

TECHNIQUE 2 – VISUALISATION

This is probably best done sitting comfortably in an armchair. If you sit fairly upright with good head support and your arms along the arms of the chair, you should be able to sit for quite a while without falling asleep or being uncomfortable.

With your eyes closed visualise a simple circle being drawn in the space in front of your closed eyes. At first it'll be a bit wobbly, but continue to practise until you can mentally draw a perfect circle. Then begin to draw the circle in other areas of your mind. You don't have to move your eyes – you can just stare straight ahead (with your eyes closed, of course) – and you have an entire universe to draw in. With practice you'll be able to draw that circle perfectly anywhere you choose.

This technique takes a lot of practice, but it's good for those of you who have strong visual appreciation. Once you've mastered the circle begin to include a cross inside it. This circle with four segments is the ancient symbol of the North American Hopi people,

who used it for exactly the same purpose as you – it is their shamanistic symbol for the universal consciousness.

Once you can draw the quartered circle perfectly and anywhere in your mind or imagination then you can progress to the pyramid. Start with a simple three-dimensional pyramid. When you have perfected it, 'hold' it for a while in your mind and rotate it. Now try to invert it. When you have mastered this you can begin to play with it – spin it round, colour it in, open it up, enlarge or shrink it, make it solid, make it transparent, make it of different materials, add two others and juggle them.

When you reach the stage when you can play with mental pyramids anytime you want, then you can begin to draw 'you'. Use the same principles and draw you anywhere you want in your mind. Begin with a simple 3-D outline. Once you can do that you can fill 'you' in, flesh you out and make you alive and breathing. Picture you standing outside of yourself. You can make yourself bigger or smaller, nearer or further away. When you have mastered this you may well find that the 'you' you are imagining is the you who is 'out'.

Some people find this technique too long to learn or too complicated or they just don't have the perseverance. Others, however, find it the only one that really works for them. It seems to appeal to artists and designers – visual, creative people.

TECHNIQUE 3 – DESIRE VISUALISATION

You can follow all the same principles as in Technique 2 but this one relies more on the visualisations of desire.

Imagine an orange sitting on a white plate. See it in your mind. Hold it there until you have examined that orange from every angle, every viewpoint. Once you can 'hold' it for a while and have really looked at it, known it and wanted it, you are allowed to mentally peel it. Use all your visualisation powers to see the skin being peeled off, see the sudden flare of orange zest as it squirts into the air, taste it. Pull back the segments and imagine one about to pop into your mouth – taste it. Let your mouth water. Let your mind taste that orange. Then let your consciousness eat that orange.

The two possibilities with this technique is that you'll either force your consciousness 'out' or you'll force your physical body to get up and find a real orange – so make sure you've got some in the house! One projector tried this technique for many weeks and reported absolutely no success at all. When questioned she admitted that she didn't like oranges and never ate them. Please use your initiative. If you don't like oranges swop the orange for a chocolate bar or a cup of fresh brewed coffee – or whatever it is that gets your taste buds going.

TECHNIQUE 4 – MOVEMENT VISUALISATION

You can follow all the same principles as in the previous two techniques, but this one relies more on the visualisations of movement.

Imagine, in your mental space, a disc. It can be any colour you like – flat and round and face-on to you. Imagine it spinning. Start it off slowly and let it build up speed. Once it has started to spin fast all the colour will bleed away and you'll have a spinning disc of pure white. Allow your imagination to go out into that spinning blur of white – let it draw you out of yourself until you are 'out'.

TECHNIQUE 5 – COUNTING BREATHS AND BEATS

Adopt the usual relaxation position described in Technique 1. This time place your left hand palm-down on your chest so that you can feel your chest rising and falling as you breathe. Bring your right hand round so that you can grasp your left hand by the wrist. Move the fingers of your right hand until you are taking your own pulse. When you can find and feel the pulse in your left wrist you are ready.

Begin by allowing yourself to relax completely. Let your breathing and heart rate slow down until they are as slow as they're going to get. Let your left hand feel your chest and count the breaths you take. When, and if, you can keep concentration until you have counted up to twenty without losing count, you'll be ready to move on to part two of this technique.

At the same time as you are counting breaths, start counting heart beats. You have to hold both counts in your head at the same time. It's difficult and you'll keep losing count or concentration.

A good tip to help you is to take a breath only every so many heart beats – try ten to begin with. Once you get into a rhythm – and this one is very difficult to begin with – you'll find that there's a curious sensation that accompanies this technique. It's as if you can feel the heart beat of the universe, or the breathing of the cosmos. Once this happens – and you'll be in a pretty deep meditative state by the time it does – it's easy to slip 'out' into the pulsating rhythm of the universe.

TECHNIQUE 6 – LUCID DREAMS

Most of us know that we have the sort of dreams where things seem real and yet we also know that we are dreaming. Well, you can induce them. A lucid dream is one where you actually wake up into your dream, and the dream can be used to spark off a projection. There are three ways to induce them.

1   If you should wake immediately after a dream of the 'normal' sort (this is best if it happens in the early hours), get out of bed at once – do not delay for a moment. Walk rapidly around your bedroom while you mentally replay the dream you've just had. Keep thinking to yourself that when you get back into bed you're going to have the same dream over again and this time you'll be awake in it. This technique has a great success rate. When you lie down to sleep you may well find yourself up and 'out' fairly quickly.

2   During the day keep thinking: 'Tonight I'm going to have a lucid dream'. Remind yourself of this all day long. And – and this is the important part – keep asking yourself during the day 'Am I dreaming now?'

This may all sound too easy, but if you can go one day without forgetting I'd be surprised. You need to develop a technique to remind you – such as writing a large 'D' on your hand with a felt-tip pen (D is for dreaming) or tying a small piece of string

72

round your little finger. Every time you see either of these two visual aids it will remind you what you're supposed to be doing.

When you get into bed hold the string or touch the 'D' as you fall asleep and, hopefully, you'll have programmed your consciousness to induce a lucid dream. Once you're in it you can be aware that a lucid dream is an attempt by the mind to rationally explain a projection. In a lucid dream you're already 'out'.

3   Set your alarm for a time in the early hours (yes, I know this one's hard). As you go to sleep recite over and over to yourself: 'When I hear the alarm I'll be out', or 'When I hear the alarm I'll have a lucid dream'. That will programme yourself in advance. You can even try banging your head on the pillow just before you go to sleep and saying, as you do so: 'I'll be lucid dreaming when the alarm goes off'. You should do this the same number of times that you've set the alarm for – set it for four o'clock and bang your head four times and repeat your instructions four times.

TECHNIQUE 7 – ENERGY RAISING

Adopt the same position as in Technique 1 – total relaxation. Once you've gone through the whole procedure you can do it again. This time, instead of imagining yourself relaxing, imagine that you are composed of pure energy. Let that energy vibrate in your imagination, slowly at first, and then gradually speeding up. Keep going back over your body checking that each part is humming. Let the energy gradually build up until you can feel your whole body vibrating very fast. You don't have to move a single muscle – this is all done in the imagination. If you find that you are actually physically moving you are doing it wrong.

When you can imagine this fast energy vibrating throughout your entire being, you can suddenly release it – direct it like an arrow – let it explode out of the top of your head in a great stream of pure consciousness – and you'll be 'out'.

TECHNIQUE 8 – CHAKRAS

According to the traditional view of yoga we have seven chakras or energy centres situated throughout the body. You can find out more about these in *Chakras for beginners* in this series. These chakras need to be fully 'open' for us to project. This technique involves opening them. They are:

1   **Base or seed chakra** – situated at the base of the spine. This chakra – called *Muladhara* – governs our instincts and genetic encoding. Its symbol is the yellow square.
2   **Pelvic chakra** – situated at the genitals and known as *Swadhistthana*. It governs our sex drive and energy. Its symbol is the white crescent.
3   **Solar plexus chakra** – situated at the navel and known as *Manipuraka*. It governs our sense of personal power and its symbol is a red triangle.
4   **Heart chakra** – situated over the heart and known as *Anahata*. It governs our emotions and its symbol is a blue hexagon.
5   **Throat chakra** – situated at the throat and known as *Vishuddha*. It governs our ability to communicate and its symbol is the white circle.
6   **Brow chakra** – situated between the eyebrows and known as *Ajna*. It governs our intellect and its symbol is the white triangle.
7   **Crown chakra** – situated on the top of the head and known as *Sahasrara*. It governs our spirituality and its symbol is a white lotus flower.

Various systems of yoga will give slightly different symbols or colours – or even names. At this stage it's not important: we are using the chakras only as a tool for projecting.

You need to lie down in the position described in Technique 1. Imagine that at each chakra you have a small bag or pouch drawn tightly shut with a draw string. Slowly visualise each chakra – starting with the base chakra – and imagine the bag being opened. Imagine the string being loosened and the bag being pulled fully open and that the chakra's symbol emerges from the bag and sits

above it. This technique opens the chakras. Once they are open – and they should be opened in the correct order starting with the base chakra and finishing with the crown chakra – there is a stream of energy released that will slowly build up from the base chakra, collecting more energy as it goes, until it emerges from the crown chakra at the top of the head. This stream of energy should carry your consciousness with it and you'll be out.

Whether you get 'out' or not, it is important to reverse the process prior to getting up again. Imagine each of the symbols being put back in the bag, and the bag being drawn tightly shut again.

TECHNIQUE 9 – FOCUS SHIFTING

This one requires you to be relaxed but fairly alert. You can lie down (Technique 1) or sit in an armchair (Technique 2). All you have to do is imagine that you are 'out'. Picture yourself a foot or two away from the physical you. Imagine that the 'you' that is 'out' is looking at the 'you' that is still in your physical body. Look at yourself and imagine every detail that you could see. Imagine how you look with your eyes shut. See your body. This technique is exactly what it says – focus shifting. You mentally shift your focus to the you that is 'out'. It is easier than it sounds but harder than you think. Once you master this technique it really is one of the best.

TECHNIQUE 10 – HEAVY/LIGHT

Lie down according to the instructions given in Technique 1. Imagine as you lie there relaxing that you are slowly becoming enormously heavy. Concentrate every fibre of your being to this one thought. You are heavier than you've ever been – feel every muscle, every limb, every part of your body weighed down with heaviness.

Just when you can tolerate no more heaviness suddenly reverse the process and imagine that you are suddenly and dramatically lighter than air. Imagine you weigh nothing at all. You may well find that your consciousness simply rises up and out.

You can liken this technique to being in a lift – you know how heavy you feel as the lift ascends rapidly and then you feel very light, as if you could float, when the lift suddenly stops.

TECHNIQUE 11 – QUESTIONING

For this one you can lie or sit. Wait until you are completely relaxed and in a dreamy state, thinking about nothing in particular. When you have reached this state you can ask questions of yourself. These are the important questions: Who am I?, What am I here for?, What is the meaning of my life?

If you ask these suddenly and with great meaning it has been found that it can so confuse your consciousness that it short-circuits and promptly leaves the physical body.

This technique seems to work best with younger people – those who are asking these questions of themselves anyway. Older people may well have worked out some answers – they may not be the right answers, but they stop the person asking any more.

TECHNIQUE 12 – TRICKERY

There are several ways to try to trick your consciousness out of your body.

- **Fast moving and stopping** – You can try running fast and then suddenly stop, and see what happens to your consciousness. It may well continue on its own for a few moments before it realises you've stopped.
- **The mirror** – Find one of those shaving mirrors which grossly magnifies. If you stand at the right distance away you can see yourself upside down. Spend some time looking at yourself and try to convince your consciousness that it is the wrong way up. Sometimes it comes out to reverse the process and put itself back where it thinks it's supposed to be.
- **Turning round** – If you stand up and remain still for a moment, and then suddenly whirl round so that you are facing the other

way, you may find your consciousness so taken by surprise that is fails to keep up with you and gets spun out.

- **Giddiness** – You can try the *Sufi* technique used by the Whirling Dervishes. Simply twirl around fast until you are completely giddy, then suddenly stop. You may fall down, so be careful, but you may also find your consciousness continues to twirl after you have stopped.

- **I'm out, you're in** – Simply concentrate hard on the thought that you are already 'out'. Convince your consciousness that it's in the wrong body – it may try to switch bodies. You don't have to use any visualisation: merely thinking about this hard enough will do the trick.

- **Hammock swinging** – If you've got a hammock you can suspend yourself upside down in it. Let yourself go completely limp and relaxed and let the hammock swing gently. You won't need much imagination to feel yourself flying. At the end of each swing try to imagine that you continue on and don't go back with the hammock. If you've got a garden with a large tree you could always try rigging up a swing from it – a large wooden board on two ropes – and lying across it face down to see what effect you can get.

- **Dream flying** – When you are going to sleep with your eyes closed just imagine that you are not touching the bed. Imagine you are completely free in space and you are dreaming and flying. It's incredible how easy this one is. Once you feel as if you are floating away, it's more than likely that you will be.

- **Being thirsty** – Before relaxing eat some salty food like crisps. Don't drink anything before projecting. Once relaxed you can imagine going to get a drink. If the thirst is strong enough you may find yourself in the kitchen trying to get a drink while still being back in your physical body. This technique isn't very pleasant, but it does seem to work sometimes.

TECHNIQUE 13 – THE FAMILIAR ROUTE

If you have a particular walk that you enjoy, then this technique is easy. Walk your walk, and as you do so, pinpoint several outstanding

features along the way that you will instantly recognise. When you are in the relaxation position walk your walk in your mind. When you come to one of your landmarks you can say to yourself: 'I am out here'.

Try walking your familiar route and mentally imagining yourself back on your bed or sitting in your armchair. You'll get so that you won't know whether you're imagining the walk or doing it in reality.

Over a period of time it's possible to be 'out' following your route almost without thinking about it.

TECHNIQUE 14 – HELPERS

We mentioned earlier that you need a support system of friends – well, now you need the friends themselves. You'll need two helpers – one to rub your ankles and feet quite vigorously, and the other to massage your forehead. They should do this with lightly clenched fists and forcefully enough to make your head tingle. This strange massage technique may well get you 'out'.

TECHNIQUE 15 – GROWING

Adopt the relaxation position on your back. When you are completely relaxed, and even a little sleepy, you can start to imagine that you are slowly changing shape – getting slightly bigger. Let yourself grow a few inches and then shrink back into your body again. Each time you try this allow yourself to grow a little more until you can fill the room with yourself. As you mentally expand so will your consciousness. Once it's filling the whole room it'll be 'out'.

TECHNIQUE 16 – KNOWING YOUR HOME

Lie down and relax. Allow your imagination to wander through your home exploring and examining every detail of every room. Try to spot something you've never noticed before – this is easier than you'd think: we rarely look that closely at anything. Once you've spotted something unusual or not previously noticed you can go and

check it out – in your physical body of course – after you've finished. It's surprising how often this one works. Sometimes we're 'out' and don't even realise it.

TECHNIQUE 17 – ARM UP

Adopt the usual relaxation position, but this time lie down and raise one arm. Keep this arm raised no matter what. As you forget what you are doing it will drop and that will remind you. The effort of keeping it up will grow intolerable after a while, and it is at this point you may well find yourself 'out' – if only to escape the discomfort.

TECHNIQUE 18 – CHILDHOOD

This one works only if you had a happy childhood, as you need to imagine you are back in your childhood home. Use your imagination to explore every room. Remember all the little details of where you once played. It's quite common for the nostalgia of such a trip to trigger something in you, and you'll find yourself 'out'. Try not to be too disappointed if you find yourself back in your childhood home and it's been redecorated – nothing stands still for ever.

TECHNIQUE 19 – AUDIO/VISUAL AIDS

One of the most successful methods of inducing an astral projection is through hypnosis. However, we don't all have a trained hypnotherapist living next door, so we must try to hypnotise ourselves. You'll need to make an audio cassette with all the relevant instructions. If you record the relaxation technique we learnt in Technique 1, you'll end up in a completely relaxed state just listening. Then you can record such instructions as: 'You are now leaving your body', or 'You feel your consciousness slowly slipping out of your physical body.'

You'll need to leave a blank space on the tape for being 'out' and then you can have instructions like: 'You are now re-entering your body,' or 'It's time to come back now.'

For getting out you could try counting yourself down: 'I'll now count down from ten to one, and when you hear 'one' you'll be out ... ten ... nine ... eight ...'

Some people find music a useful tool for projecting – others find it a distraction. If you find it easy to get lost in music you could try projecting while listening to something suitable. Rachmaninov's *Symphony No. 2* has been found to be useful. There are many 'New Age' tapes on the market and many of these are suitable. Try to avoid any that may distract you with unexpected noises like sudden rainfall or whale songs. The Japanese composer, Kitaro, has produced several cassettes that have been found to be most helpful for this type of experience. Try his album *Silk Road*.

You could try staring at a *yantra*. A yantra is a complex pattern that draws the eye in and enables you to get lost in the design. Many New Age shops sell them either as posters or cards. They 'hold the mind' and, by staring at them, you can find your consciousness slipping into them, through them, and 'out'.

You could try using a *mantra* – a repeated phrase or word that you say over and over again to yourself internally. Try 'I am astrally projecting now', or 'I am out'. Whatever phrase you use it should be short, positive and meaningful. It's no point saying 'I'll be projecting in a minute', or 'I think I'm projecting'. You have to be firm with yourself.

TECHNIQUE 20 – MEDITATION

There are several meditation techniques that achieve successful results.

- **Visible breath** – Relax and allow yourself to be completely at peace. Concentrate on your breathing until it is slow, shallow and regular. You may like to try this by breathing in through your nose and out through your mouth.

  As you breathe imagine that you can see your breath leaving your mouth. Imagine it as a white misty stream. Imagine that this breath contains your consciousness and, as you breath out, so your consciousness is leaving your physical body.

- **Abdominal breathing** – Bring your breath down so that you are breathing using your abdomen. You can rest your hands on your abdomen and feel your stomach gently rising and falling. As you feel the rhythm you can imagine your consciousness swelling and retracting with each breath. Imagine your consciousness swelling and rising beyond your physical body and into the surrounding air. With each breath imagine it going a little further.
- **Third-eye meditation** – Relax with your eyes closed and imagine that there is a spot of light within your mind situated just above your eyebrows in the centre of your forehead and about an inch inside your head. This is the location of your third eye – the pineal gland. You can concentrate on this tiny spot of light and imagine it as your consciousness. Let it expand until it fills your whole mind and see what happens. You may find that this dot of light changes colour and shape, and develops patterns. It may well change to a pulsating ball of dark blue. By concentrating on this ball of blue you may find it possible to encourage your consciousness to move with it, and move outside of the physical you.
- **Closed circle meditation** – As you relax allow your body to feel like a ball of energy. Use your imagination to see your consciousness right in the centre of this ball. Let your imagination allow your consciousness to expand until it fills the ball, and then let it overspill. Imagine your body being surrounded by the aura – a misty envelope of energy all around you. Let this aura expand until it is several feet from you and your consciousness fills it.
- **Vibration meditation** – You need to be sitting in your armchair for this one. Sit and become relaxed with your hands lightly folded in your lap. When you are completely relaxed you can begin to rock gently backwards and forwards. You'll quickly find that you'll discover your own 'rhythm'. This rocking should be barely perceptible. When you have found your rhythm and feel at ease with this rocking, you can begin to speed it up. As you go faster and faster you may find that your consciousness is unable to 'keep up' and is being trailed slightly behind each movement. Once you can feel this shift – your consciousness is actually out of sync with you – you'll be able to push it further and further until it is out.

TECHNIQUE 21 – ALTERED VIEWPOINT

You know how it is when you're a child – you crawl under tables, climb on the furniture, make camps under the beds. Well, as an adult we stop doing this, but this technique allows you to play again. Get a chair (or a step ladder is best if you can trust yourself to use one without falling off it) and put it in the furthermost corner of your bedroom. Stand on the chair and see your bed from an altered viewpoint. Have you ever seen your bed from this angle before? Your viewpoint should be higher than usual. Imagine yourself lying in bed. What would you look like? Could you imagine being 'out' and seeing yourself from this angle?

This technique works best if you can get as high as possible. Study this new viewpoint until you know it well. When you're ready, go and lie down on the bed and close your eyes and imagine that you're back standing on the chair, or whatever, and looking down at yourself. You may well find you are.

TECHNIQUE 22 – SKY BATHING
AND STAR GAZING

Try lying on your back out of doors for these techniques. If you can, find a hill where you can lie on the top and thus not see any surrounding countryside. Go through the usual relaxation routine, but keep your eyes open. Stare straight up at the sky – a warm cloudy day is best. As you look up, imagine that you are floating free looking down. This technique should obviously be practised somewhere where you'll be undisturbed. Someone walking up to you or a puppy jumping on you would be terribly distracting, and could even be quite a shock if you were 'out'.

You can try the same technique on a warm starry evening. Looking up at the stars you can imagine you are up amongst them floating free. Imagine you are looking down at your physical body. You can extend this technique – try it lying in a boat idly drifting down a gentle river, or if you are a passenger in a car, or on a train.

WHAT HAPPENS NEXT?

I guess that these should be enough techniques for you to be getting on with. There may be more that I've not come across. You may like to experiment with your own. See how you get on. Remember that some of the techniques require considerable patience and training. Don't expect immediate results and don't get frustrated or disappointed if nothing happens for a while.

Astral projection can become a life-long interest. You can practise every night when you go to sleep – or make it a special thing you do occasionally. You may like to talk to friends about this and try to meet up with them when you're 'out' – or compare results.

You can try to keep a projection diary. As soon as you wake in the morning write down anything at all that you may remember about your experiences while asleep. Do it immediately. The human consciousness works like a computer – you have RAM and ROM memory – and short-term memory is exactly that – short term. If you don't write down your dreams and experiences at once you'll have forgotten them within minutes.

You may like to write down any experiences you have and send them to me, via the publishers, and we may be able to use them in a future publication. You can also send me any other techniques you discover. But I cannot answer any questions – I don't know all the answers and anyway you have to find out some things for yourself. Good luck and see you out there!

CASE HISTORIES

REG

I had what they call an out of the body experience when I was in my late teens. I'd been to a party and was very drunk. When I tried to sleep all I got was the whirling-pit effect. Next thing I knew, I was out of my body and floating above myself. Funny thing was, I wasn't drunk any more. I was so knocked out by the whole thing I wanted

to learn how to do it again. I went to the library and read all I could on astral projection. All the books I read said that it was all quite normal and lots of people could do it, although I'd never heard of it before. Some of the methods of doing it deliberately seemed a bit involved, but I tried one way where you had to relax and go into this sort of trance. You had to cross your arms over your chest and cross your ankles while lying down. Then you had to concentrate on this spot inside your forehead and let your breathing go really light, as if you were barely breathing, like being asleep I suppose. Anyway I don't think I've ever really maanged to get out again, but I'm not sure. I've often fallen asleep while I've been trying this and I'm sure I'm out, but you only know when you're awake again and then you don't think so. I've had lots of dreams where I was flying and I know I left my body. I often get quite excited and say to myself that I must remember this when I wake up. I usually don't when I first wake up, but sometime during the day I'll be stopped by the thought that I was out. I'm still practising because I love the feeling that I have some sort of control over it.

John

My girlfriend, Sarah, and I have been practising astral projection for a couple of years now. Every night when we go to sleep we lay on our backs next to each other and hold hands. We're trying to meet up on the astral plane. We've both had experiences of getting out, but never together. I once felt myself leaving my body through my third eye and found myself floating up by the ceiling. I could see Sarah's body and it was all shimmery and light. I think she was getting ready to come out or just going back in. I got excited because I thought it was going to work and was whisked back in pretty fast. Lots of times I can feel myself leaving, but you can't help feeling exhilarated and then you can't go anywhere. It's a sort of catch 22 situation – you get excited because it's exciting but you can only do it if you're really calm. We've had some amazing dreams where we've virtually had the same dream – that's happened quite often. Or we'll have some common theme in a dream, although what happens might be different. I'm glad I've got someone who also likes this stuff because it would be weird trying this and not being able to talk about it to anyone.

HILLARY

I'm not sure I really practise any techniques as such, but I did get into aromatherapy a little while ago and started taking baths by candlelight. You add the oils to your bathwater and let yourself really relax. I don't know if it's the flickering of the candles or just the warmth and general relaxation, but there's been a couple of times when I suddenly can't feel anything at all and I'm sure I'm lying above my body. I like the feeling, but if it goes on too long I hate the shock when you sort of wake up or come round or come back or whatever and you suddenly feel how cold the water is. Ugh, that really is horrid. I don't know if I would do this at any other time but I like the feeling I get in the bath.

MOLLY

I'm not sure you need books on this – surely everyone knows about it and how to do it, don't they? All I have to do is remember the house I was brought up in. I visualise every room, especially the kitchen and my bedroom, and invariably I find myself back there. The house has changed a bit but not a lot. I've never seen anyone else there, though, and I've never been back to check that it has changed but I love wandering around in it. I haven't been back to Gloucester since I was quite young but I can remember everything about living there.

GARY

Once you discover your own particular way of astral projection it's quite easy. I've several friends who all try to and we all have a different method. Each of us has different results, sometimes it's easy and other times it's hard. My own personal method is to shout at myself. Do you remember that bit in *Wind in the Willows* where mole is lost in the wild wood and the rabbit runs towards him and says: 'get out of this, you fool, get out'? Well, that's exactly what I shout to myself. It quite often works, especially if I surprise myself with it, usually just as I'm falling asleep. I don't go anywhere, just rise up above the bed and hang there for a bit, but it's an amazing experience, sort of really frees up your head if you know what I

mean – answers a lot of questions about soul and death and such like. Once you've done it everything all seems to make sense. I don't know how the Church can carry on talking such nonsense when we can all try this and see for ourselves.

Malcolm

Sometimes I think all these terms, like astral projection, seem to blur together. I don't practise anything like what you'd call techniques, but I have meditated for years. I started off with TM and have now progressed to Zen. The experiences I've had seem to be very similar to what you've described. I can sit for up to eight hours meditating, and during that time there will often be moments when I know I'm watching myself. I've even had the feeling that there's several 'me's' all watching me. If you go with it then it feels fine but if you fight it or question it I think it would drive you mad. It's all fine though. I don't know or care what any of it means or what it's called, I just know that I'm being shown some amazing things about myself and the universe around me.

Carol

All I do is imagine I'm downstairs in the kitchen making tea or something and wake up, and I am but I know I'm still asleep upstairs in bed. I only do it for fun sometimes. I don't make tea, of course, as you can't move or lift anything. I once did it and found myself downstairs in what I call my 'astral body' and I was completely naked. My brother came in and I shrieked although he couldn't see me. I was suddenly back in bed and I was wearing my pyjamas again. That made me laugh after a while but it put me off for a bit.

June

When I was in hospital having my first child I had to have a Caesarean and they did it under a general because I was pretty ill. Or at least I think it was a general but it may have been merely heavy sedation. The weird thing is that I was conscious for the whole time and heard and saw everything. It was only later when I

remembered it all that I realised that not only could I see the birth but I could see me as well. That freaked me for a while I can tell you. I mean how can you be you and still be another you. Then I read this article about Near Death Experiences and realised that was what I had gone through. Someone lent me a book about it and I've been trying to do it again. I don't know if I use any particular method. I just sort of lie down and will it to happen. Sometimes I can feel myself beginning to go but I never seem to make it. But once you feel that initial lift-off you know it's possible – and that's what makes you keep trying. Even if you never manage to do it, there's still enough going on to make you want to try again.

BEN

I listen to music. If you select the right piece it's easy to get lost in it and just drift away. I often find myself walking through landscapes that I've never seen before, or been to. I've never seen anyone else or my own body. I have no idea how it happens or how to do it, but it happens often enough that I can sort of plan it. You have to make sure there's absolutely no way you'll be disturbed. If you even think someone could come in it won't happen. I suppose that's a sort of defence thing.

COLIN

It happens to me a lot in lifts. As soon as the lift starts to go up I stay where I am and the lift goes on without me – but only for a tiny bit before I catch up. I once managed to stay where I was for long enough to see underneath the lift. In the office block where I work the lift is quite fast, and if you get in early enough in the mornings you can go right to the top floor without it stopping to let anyone in. That usually does the trick. It doesn't happen on the way down though.

VICKY

If you lie in bed and tense yourself up all over really tight and then suddenly let go, you have this weird feeling that you're not inside you any more. Sometimes I have to do it many times and for quite a

while before I get the effect. I don't know why I do it, it's just a strange sensation that I really like. I've never seen my own body or 'floated' or anything. I just seem to leak out a bit round the edges. My boyfriend once caught me doing it and I had to explain what I was doing. He thought I was a bit odd. He's an 'ex' now, anyway.

CATHERINE

I tried it a couple of times and didn't have any success at all. My friend's really into all this stuff and she said it was easy. Every time I tried it, I fell asleep.

ROBERT

I used to do a lot of yoga when I was young but gave it up. Recently I wanted to start again, so I thought I'd see if I could still do a headstand. Well, I could but I also had this feeling that I was falling out of my head. It felt like I was melting into a puddle on to the floor. I didn't like the feeling and it's put me off trying again.

JAMIE

I think I've tried most of the ways of astral projection – some work and most don't. I find the easiest is to roll your eyes back as far as they will go and hold them there. If you keep up the pressure, you'll get blinding bursts of light and it sparks off a projection. I have spoken to lots of other people about this and no one else seems to be able to use this method. I can sometimes project if I lie down in a completely dark room on the floor, but it has to be utterly black so you can't see any light. If you keep your eyes open and stare straight ahead it seems to work. Once you find yourself out and up above your own body, the whole room is filled with light and you can see everything. I usually just zip around the room and back in again. I always plan great journeys, but the second I'm out I can't be bothered going anywhere – there's no point.

USEFUL
INFORMATION

FURTHER READING

S. J. Blackmore, *Beyond the Body: an Investigation of Out-of-Body Experiences*, Heinemann, 1982.

J. H. Brennan, *Understanding Reincarnation*, Aquarian Press, 1990.

Robert Crookall, *The Study and Practice of Astral Projection*, Aquarian Press, 1961.

— *The Techniques of Astral Projection*, Aquarian Press, 1964.

— *More Astral Projections*, Aquarian Press, 1964.

— *The Mechanics of Astral Projection*, Darshana International, India, 1969.

— *Out Of The Body Experiences*, University Books, NY, 1970.

O. Fox, *Astral Projection*, University Books Inc., 1962.

Richard L. Gregory, *The Oxford Companion to the Mind*, Oxford University Press, 1987.

Liz Hodgkinson, *The Personal Growth Handbook*, Piatkus, 1993.

R. A. Monroe, *Journeys Out of the Body*, Doubleday, 1971.

S. Muldoon and H. Carrington, *The Projection of the Astral Body*, Rider, 1929.

— *The Phenomena of Astral Projection*, Rider, 1951.

John D. Ralphs, *Exploring the Fourth Dimension*, Quantum, 1992.

D. S. Rogo, *The Out-Of-Body Experiences*, Penguin, 1978.

M. Sabom, *Recollections of Death*, Harper & Row, 1982.

S. Smith, *The Enigma of Out-Of-Body Travel*, Garrett Publications, 1965.

C. T. Tart, *Out-of-the-Body Experiences*, G. P. Putnams, New York, 1974.
Brian Ward, ESP – *The Sixth Sense*, Macdonald Guidelines, 1977.
G. D. Wassermann, *Shadow Matter*, Mandrake of Oxford, 1993.
L. Watson, *The Romeo Error*, Coronet, 1976.

Useful addresses

United Kingdom

College of Psychic Studies
16 Queensbury Place
London
SW7 2EB
Study of mediums and spirit communication.

Institute of Parascience
Sprytown
Lifton
Devon
PL1 0AY
Research into the paranormal.

International Association for Near-Death Studies
PO Box 193
London
SW1K 9JZ
Research into near-death experiences.

The Natural Death Centre
20 Heber Road
London
NW2 6AA
Researches NDEs and alternatives to euthanasia.

Paraphysical Laboratory
Downtown
Wiltshire
Information and research on paraphysics.